Statistics and Performance Measures for Public Library Networked Services

JOHN CARLO BERTOT

CHARLES R. McCLURE

JOE RYAN

AMERICAN LIBRARY ASSOCIATION

Chicago and London   2001

While extensive effort has gone into ensuring the reliability of information appearing in this book, the publisher makes no warranty, express or implied, on the accuracy or reliability of the information, and does not assume and hereby disclaims any liability to any person for any loss or damage caused by errors or omissions in this publication.

Design and composition by The Publishing Services Group

Printed on 50-pound white offset, a pH-neutral stock, and bound in 10-point cover stock by Documation

The paper used in this publication meets the minimum requirements of American National Standard for Information Sciences—Permanence of Paper for Printed Library Materials, ANSI Z39.48-1992. ∞

Printed in the United States of America.

05 04 03 02 01   5 4 3 2 1

DEDICATION

The authors dedicate this book to the memory of Jeffrey Katzer, a professor and Associate Dean of the School of Information Studies, Syracuse University, who died in March 2000. Jeffrey had a most distinguished record at the School of Information Studies, having come to Syracuse University in 1969, starting the doctoral program, directing the research work of many doctoral students, and mentoring many of the faculty.

To a large extent, the soul of the School of Information Studies was personalized by Jeffrey's dedication and commitment to the school and to the profession. He served as the catalyst that kept the school in a state of ongoing innovative development and excitement. His ability to work with everyone, to expect excellence in everything we did, and his sense of humor helped to make the School of Information Studies one of the greatest programs of information studies in the world.

Jeffrey's influence on the training and education of a host of doctoral students over the years cannot be overemphasized. His stance toward the importance of research in information studies and the need for information studies faculty to take an active and ongoing role in research permeated the School of Information Studies. He understood the importance and role of a professional school and the need for research to be useful for practitioners. We continue to feel his influence as we complete this project and start others.

Jeffrey embraced the challenge of teaching the use of numbers in decision making, their strengths and limits, to librarians and teachers of librarians—a challenge not unlike the one we faced as we set out to write this work. Two of us were his students. His approach was to set high standards and be generous when they weren't always achieved. He taught us that while capturing illusive truth is measurement's goal, reducing error in measurement is equally important. Good researchers, like Jeffrey, were agile, subtle, and sometimes profound as they strived to accomplish these two goals.

Jeffrey was friend, colleague, research partner, mentor, bridge partner, humorist, and statesman. His ongoing support and encouragement to be "as good as you can be" affected many of us. His influence on all of us, in various ways, is significant and continuous. He brought a sense of passion and excitement to the School of Information Studies that spread to everyone. We, and many others, were fortunate to have known him and to have had him as a friend, colleague, and mentor.

John Carlo Bertot
Charles R. McClure
Joe Ryan

CONTENTS

3 Recommended Composite and Performance Measures

4 User Assessment

7   Extending the Use of Statistics and Measures for the Networked Environment   75

APPENDIXES

ACKNOWLEDGMENTS

The authors are indebted to a number of individuals who contributed to this project and, ultimately, the publication of this manual. First, the authors acknowledge the research award from the Institute for Museum and Library Services (IMLS) in 1998 to support the study *Developing Public Library Statistics and Performance Measures for the Networked Environment* (grant no. LL-80102). That study led directly to the writing of the manual presented here.

We also wish to thank the state librarians and state library staff at Utah, North Carolina, Pennsylvania, Michigan, Maryland, and Delaware for also supporting the study. These six state library agencies contributed both resources and staff to allow the study team to conduct a range of in-depth on-site visits and other data collection efforts to test the various statistics and performance measures described in the manual.

Within these and other states, a number of public librarians agreed to work directly with the study team to identify their needs and uses for statistics and measures to describe the networked environment; to test and refine the proposed statistics and measures; and to explain to the study team various strengths, weaknesses, and potential uses of the statistics and measures. The range of people "in the trenches," who offered valuable ideas, suggestions, and insights is extensive. We especially appreciate the assistance of the field-test liaisons: Jane Gill, Karen Sherrard, Anne Silvers Lee, and David Wilson.

While we cannot list all the participants here, their assistance was essential to the completion of the study and the writing of the manual.

We also gratefully acknowledge the assistance and input from members of the project's advisory committee. These included: Amy Owen, Jim Fish, Timothy Owens, Barbara W. Cole, Keith Curry Lance, Barbara G. Smith, Joey Rodger, Douglas Zweizig, Mary Jo Lynch, Tom Sloan, Janet Laverty, Maurice Travillian, Gerry Rowland, Beverly Choltco-Devlin, Naomi Krefman, Keith Lance, Sandy Cooper, Martin Dillon, Douglas Abrams, Michael Osborne, and Mary Lou Caskey. We especially appreciate their time and effort to meet with us at various conferences, to offer ideas and suggestions, and to review various drafts of the manual.

We also wish to acknowledge a number of people who were part of the study team over the project's duration. We especially want to thank Colleen Ostiguy, research assistant at SUNY Albany, for all her hard work on the project, for managing the project web site and handling a range of logistical issues, always with good humor.

While the authors gratefully acknowledge all the various folks who contributed to the success of the project and the completion of the manual, the responsibility for the content of the manual belongs to the authors. As indicated in the manual itself, there is still considerable room for debate, discussion, and ongoing evolution of the statistics and measures presented here. We look forward to working with others to continue this evolution.

John Carlo Bertot
Charles R. McClure
Joe Ryan

1

Introduction

Public libraries face challenging times in the new millennium as they consider which services to provide through what medium. The digital revolution offers public libraries many opportunities—opportunities coupled with a number of management and planning issues. With the thought, consideration, and devotion inherent in the profession, public librarians must take action, meet these challenges, and resolve new issues in the evolving networked environment.

One particular issue that needs attention is that of measuring network-based library services and resources. Public libraries increasingly provide and use network-based services and resources such as online databases, web sites, and online reference. Measuring the usage of these services and resources is important, as such data can:

- Assist public library staff in resource allocation, management, and planning activities;
- Provide, if collected nationally, regional, state, and national public library network usage data for peer comparisons, benchmarking, and aggregate usage information;
- Serve as a means to evaluate public library networked services;
- Present the extent and nature of public library networked activities to the community the library serves; and

- Improve the political and funding climate for public libraries in the community.

This manual offers public librarians, State Library agencies, and policy makers a beginning set of network statistics and performance measures to measure network-based services and resources. The manual, the first of its kind, is an initial effort in offering public librarians assistance in developing, maintaining, and reporting network statistics and performance measures.

THE CURRENT CONTEXT

Public libraries traditionally use the benchmarks of circulation and walk-ins as indicators of library services usage. In many instances, however, public libraries are experiencing a decrease in use in these critical areas of services measures (see Figure 1-1). And yet, public libraries overall have increased dramatically the services that they provide in the networked environment by subscribing to online databases, developing web pages and web sites, digitizing collections, training users to use computers and the Internet, and a host of other services—none of which are captured in current data collection efforts. Without the development, collection, analysis, and reporting of electronic resource and service measures, public libraries are misrepresenting their overall service usage and potentially damaging their

FIGURE 1-1   Current Public Library Services Context

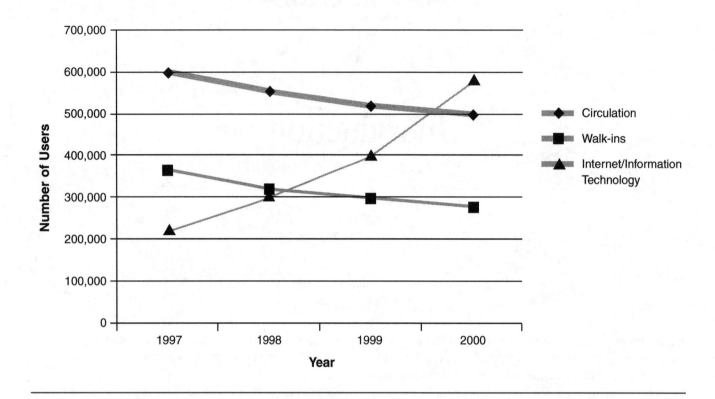

ability to compete for scarce funding resources in their communities.

The statistics and performance measures in this manual are designed to assist public libraries to present their services picture to the communities that they serve. While the manual focuses on electronic resources and services statistics and performance measures, the data collection efforts of public libraries will need to combine existing and more traditional data collection activities with those proposed in this manual to best reflect current library services usage.

Manual Goals

The overall goals of this manual are to assist public librarians to:

- Establish a core set of network national statistics and performance measures that describe public library use of the Internet and web-based services and resources;
- Measure a library's network-based resources and services;

- Use the statistics and performance measures to describe library network service and resource usage to various audiences;
- Incorporate measuring library network usage measures into ongoing library services measurement activities; and
- Develop an overall picture of network service and resource usage in their libraries.

The manual, therefore, seeks to provide public librarians and State Library agencies with network statistical and performance measurement guidelines that begin at the local library level and aggregate to form a national system of network statistics and performance measures.

Why This Manual?

While there are a number of efforts in progress to assist public libraries to develop electronic resources and services measures, these efforts lack coordination, agreement in approach, and an overall vision for public library electronic resources and services measurement in general. This manual serves to:

- **Ensure that public libraries engage in standard measurement activities.** Data collection efforts and measurement activities gain in utility if every library measures the same services and resources in the same manner. This manual provides standard definitions and procedures that have gone through substantial field-testing for the statistics and measures it recommends.

- **Describe what libraries actually do.** Given the context of decreased circulation and patron visits, how is it that public librarians indicate that they are busier than ever? Libraries need to find ways that better reflect their actual resource and services usage, especially in the networked environment.

- **Remove the reliance on gut sentiment.** In the competitive context of dwindling resources, it no longer is sufficient to *say* that libraries and librarians are busy. Rather, there is a need for a standardized measurement approach that provides hard evidence that this is the case to sustain the public library's digital transformation.

- **Instruct staff.** A key component to collecting data about public library electronic resources and services use is a staff that understands the statistics and the context in which they occur. This manual provides a beginning point for instruction on collecting, analyzing, and using electronic resources and services data.

- **Reeducate public library governing boards.** While the networked environment is new in many ways to public libraries and librarians, it is newer still to the governing boards on which public libraries rely for advice and funding support. Governing board members need instruction on the use and interpretation of measures of electronic resources and services.

- **Assist librarians to interpret the results.** A key aspect of statistical measurement is that of interpretation and presentation of results. This manual provides librarians with assistance in understanding the statistics and measures, analyzing the data, and interpreting the results of the analyzed data.

- **Assist librarians to work with vendors.** With the advent of online vendor-based services, public libraries no longer control vast amounts of critical usage data. For example, public libraries will need to rely on vendors to report back online database usage statistics. This manual begins the process of clarifying library needs from vendors and builds common consensus as negotiations with vendors about data reporting continue.

- **Remain fleet-footed in measuring electronic resources and services.** The networked environment is one of rapid change. Thus, measuring the use of electronic resources and services will need to adapt continually to keep pace with technology. This manual lays the foundation for *current* measures of electronic resources and services and a process to modify old and develop new measures as technology changes the nature and implementation of library resources and services.

What This Manual Is Not

While this manual serves to inform public librarians as to the types of statistics and measures to collect in the networked environment, the ways in which to capture such statistics and measures, and the facilitation of the interpretation of such statistics and measures, this manual does not:

- **Supplant traditional measurement activities.** The statistics and measures contained in the manual do not replace traditional measures of library resources and services. Indeed, it is best to view the statistics and measures in this manual as part of a larger data collection effort that captures overall library resources and services usage.

- **Replace thinking.** While the authors would like to provide public librarians with a magic measurement bullet, we cannot. A well-executed data collection program requires thought, effort, and work in the trenches to bear fruit. This manual is a first comprehensive step for electronic resources and services measurement activities, but only that. Users of the manual will get out of it what they put into it in terms of making arguments for more staff or the reallocation of existing staff, new resources, redefinition of success, proof of use, and many others.

- **Provide the final word.** Measuring electronic resources and services is the equivalent of hitting a fast-moving target. The statistics and measures provided in this manual may have a limited shelf life of three to five years at most. Thus, the library profession is now entering a measurement world that requires continual modification and development efforts.

- **Provide measures with absolute accuracy.** As explained below, this manual took pains to develop statistics and measures that provide as accurately as possible electronic resources and services statistics and measures. They are, however, *estimates* of the usage of the resources and services they measure. Participants in the development process for the statistics and measures in this manual consider rigorous estimates better than what currently exists—nothing. This manual, therefore, attempts to carry out the possible, not the ideal.

- **Offer all possible statistics and measures of electronic resources and services.** Throughout the development process of the statistics and measures contained in this manual, there were suggestions for numerous potentially useful measures. After much deliberation, field-testing, and revision, the statistics and measures in this manual reflect a core set of usage measures that *all* public library systems can collect in part or in toto. As the electronic measurement needs of libraries change, so too will the statistics and measures they need to collect.

- **Provide measures of non-Internet-based resources and services.** This manual attempts to reflect current and near-future library electronic services and resources. While there are libraries that still provide CD-ROM services, for example, libraries are increasingly migrating the electronic services and resources to the Internet. Thus, this manual recommends statistics and measures that capture Internet-based resources and services.

Given the above, librarians should view this manual as part of a larger ongoing planning and evaluation process such as those reflected in *Output Measures for Public Libraries* (Van House et al., 1987*), Planning for Results: A Public Library Transformation Process* (Himmel and Wilson, 1998), *Managing For Results: Effective Resource Allocation for Public Libraries* (Nelson, Altman, and Mayo, 2000), and *Wired for the Future* (Mayo and Nelson, 1999).

METHODOLOGY

The study team used a multimethod approach to develop the statistics, performance measures, data collection techniques, and suggestions offered in this manual. The effort encompassed a variety of data collection activities that involved library researchers, practitioners, policy makers, State Library agencies, and public library

administrators and staff. In particular, the study team worked with public libraries, State Library agencies, library consortia, and library-based statewide networks in six states throughout the data collection process (Delaware, Maryland, Michigan, North Carolina, Pennsylvania, and Utah). The study team based the selection of these states on the following criteria:

- Willingness to participate in a multiphase and longitudinal data collection effort;
- Ability to provide the study team feedback on various study data collection instruments and efforts;
- Ability to inform the study team of the issues identified in collecting network statistics and performance measures;
- Diversity of network resources and services implementation within the State Library and public libraries throughout the state; and
- Willingness to spearhead network statistics and performance measure adoption efforts, first in their states, and then on the national level.

The states, therefore, served as study advisors, participants, and test beds.

As test beds, public libraries, State Library agencies, statewide library-based networks, and library consortia assisted in the development of both the statistics and performance measures contained in this manual. They also served as field-test agents for the statistics and performance measures during January and February 2000. These participants provided invaluable feedback throughout the development and field-testing phases of the statistics and measures in terms of the definition, methodology, level of effort, benefit, and utility of the statistics and measures.

A separate, but important aspect, of the study involved participation of various online database vendors. The data collected and maintained by them are an integral part of the public library network services and resources picture, but are not collected or maintained by the libraries or state networks or consortia. As such, through the field-test participants, the study team contacted and worked with a number of database vendors to assess various database usage data.

Together, these data collection approaches and activities yielded the network statistics and performance measures contained in this manual. They also helped the study team to identify key issues in the collection, maintenance, and dissemination of the statistics and performance measures.

QUALIFICATIONS AND LIMITATIONS REVISITED

This manual serves as a beginning point for the development, collection, and reporting of public library network statistics and performance measures. In using the manual, librarians need to consider the following:

- The statistics and performance measures contained in this manual may not apply to all libraries. For example, not all public libraries provide online reference services or subscribe to online databases;

- The statistics and performance measures are best viewed as *estimates* of network usage. The data collection techniques, methodologies, and definitions, while tested, modified, and retested in several different ways, are not so precise as to provide absolute precision in measurement;

- The statistics and performance measures are evolutionary and will need to change over time to better reflect the technologies, data collection techniques, and other issues of the future; and

- *Some* measurement is better than *no* measurement. The increasing reliance of public libraries on networks to provide and access library services and resources necessitates the adoption of some base line statistics and performance measures.

As such, this manual assists public librarians, State Library agencies, policy makers, trustees, and researchers to initiate a systematic data collection system for library network services and resources.

USING THE MANUAL

Chapter 2 of the manual presents the recommended electronic resource and services statistics including definitions, procedures for collection, and suggestions for potential use. Chapter 3 makes use of the proposed electronic resource and services statistics by combining them, often with traditional measures such as circulation, to form composite measures or by creating ratios to form performance measures. Chapter 4 discusses various techniques through which to capture user-based information. Chapter 5 discusses managing the electronic resources and services data collection and analysis process. Chapter 6 raises a set of issues to consider should you need to develop new measures of electronic resources and services in the future because of advances in information technology or local need. Chapter 7 concludes with a number of observations, issues, and future directions for network usage measurement activities.

The manual does not review other library network statistics and performance measure projects or literature. Readers wishing to review additional literature should consult the project web site <http://www.ii.fsu.edu> for pointers to a number of resources and references on the topic, as well as the appendixes in this manual for selected citations.

2

Recommended Statistics

This chapter presents the recommended statistics useful to begin measuring electronic resources and services offered by public libraries. Each statistic description includes: a definition, indication of who should collect it, survey period, procedures for collection, special considerations (if appropriate), and analysis and use. Figure 2-1 presents the recommended statistics in summary form. Chapter 3 illustrates how to combine these recommended statistics, often with such traditional measures as circulation, to produce composite measures or how to divide these statistics to create performance measures. Appendix A contains additional statistics and measures that local libraries may want to consider for possible use.

RECOMMENDED STATISTICS

Public Access Internet Workstations

Number of public access Internet workstations

Definition: Annual count of the number of library owned public access graphical workstations that connect to the Internet for a dedicated purpose (to access an OPAC or specific database) or multiple purposes. Workstations may include personal computers, "thin clients," graphical terminals, dedicated workstations, or networked computers if connected to the Internet and publicly accessible. Library owned includes worksta-

tions that are: purchased by the library, donated to the library, or controlled by the library. The workstations need not be physically on the library premises; for example, the count would include a library kiosk providing Internet access at a local mall.

Collected by: Library collects.

Survey Period: Measure once annually.

Procedure: Count the number of graphical workstations with Internet access (no matter the speed or type of connection) that are available to the public as of the annual date chosen. The library may find a form like Figure 2-2 helpful for data collection.

Count the number of workstations reported on the work form here and the highest bandwidth below; see "Maximum Bandwidth of Public Access Internet Workstations."

Special Considerations: Exclude workstations that could be configured to connect to the Internet but are not connected at the time of the count. For example, exclude a workstation on the library network that could be connected to the Internet (using the library network) but has been dedicated to accessing a popular CD-ROM title. Do not count workstations that may be connected to the Internet after the annual date chosen. Do not count workstations that provide text only access to the Internet.

FIGURE 2-1   Electronic Resources and Services Statistics

Proposed National Statistic	Definition
Public Access Internet Workstations	
Number of public access Internet workstations	Annual count of the number of library owned public access graphical workstations that connect to the Internet for a dedicated purpose (to access an OPAC or specific database) or multiple purposes.
Number of public access Internet workstation users	Annual count of the number of users of all of the library's graphical public access workstations connected to the Internet computed from a one-week sample.
Maximum speed of public access Internet workstations	Indication of the maximum bandwidth of public Internet access, e.g., less than 56kbps, 56kbps, 128kbps, 1.5mbps, etc.
Electronic Services	
Number of virtual reference transactions	Annual count of the number of reference transactions using the Internet. A transaction must include a question received electronically (e.g., via e-mail, WWW form, etc.) *and* responded to electronically (e.g., e-mail).
Number of staff hours spent servicing information technology *Report:* Information technology staff, paid public service staff (professional librarian, paraprofessional), volunteer, and total	Annual count of the staff hours spent in servicing information technology in public service areas based on a one-week sample.
Databases	
Number of full-text titles available by subscription *Report:* Serial titles, other titles, total titles	Count of the number of full-text titles that the library subscribes to and offers to the public computed one time annually.
Number of database sessions	Total count of the number of sessions (logins) initiated to the online databases. Definition adapted from proposed International Coalition of Library Consortia (ICOLC) standard <http://www.library.yale.edu/consortia/webstats.html>.
Number of database queries/searches	Total count of the number of searches conducted in the library's online databases. Subsequent activities by users (e.g., browsing, printing) are not considered part of the search process. Definition adapted from proposed ICOLC standard <http://www.library.yale.edu/consortia/webstats.html>.
Number of items examined using subscription services	Count of the number of views to each entire host to which the library subscribes. A view is defined as the number of full-text articles/ pages, abstracts, citations, and text only, text/graphics viewed. Definition adapted from proposed ICOLC standard <http://www.library.yale.edu/consortia/webstats.html>.

(continued)

FIGURE 2-1 Electronic Resources and Services Statistics (continued)

Proposed National Statistic	Definition
Virtual Visits	
Number of virtual visits to networked library resources *Report:* Number of internal virtual visits, number of external virtual visits, number of total virtual visits	Count of visits to the library via the Internet. A *visit* occurs when an external user connects to a networked library resource for any length of time or purpose (regardless of the number of pages or elements viewed). Examples of a networked library resource include a library OPAC or a library web page. In the case of a user visit to a library web site a user who looks at 16 pages and 54 graphic images registers one visit on the web server.
Instruction	
User information technology instruction *Report:* Number of users instructed, number of hours of instruction	A count of the number of users instructed and the hours of instruction offered in the use of information technology or resources obtainable using information technology in structured, informal, and electronically delivered instruction sessions conducted or sponsored by the library.
Staff information technology instruction *Report:* Number of staff instructed, number of hours of staff instruction	Annual count of the total number of staff instructed and the number of hours of formal instruction in the management or use of information technology or resources obtainable using information technology.

FIGURE 2-2 Public Access Internet Workstation Inventory Work Form

Workstation ID	Location	Type of Connection (e.g., dialup, ISDN, fiber optic, frame relay, cable modem, satellite)	Bandwidth (e.g., less than 56kbps, 56kbps, 64-128kbps, more than 128kbps but less than 1.5mbps, 1.5mbps, more than 1.5mbps)	Purchase Date

Computers in any public area of the library (e.g., adult, children's, computer labs, etc.) if graphical and connected to the Internet should be counted. Count public access, graphical, Internet-connected workstations shared by both staff and the public if available for use by the public for at least half of the hours during an average week that the library is open to the public. Workstations used by the staff only should *not* be counted. Reference desk computers used by staff to assist the public should *not* be counted.

Analysis and Use: The statistic for the number of public access Internet workstations is a basic measure of library input. The assumption is that the number of public access Internet workstations is a useful indicator of the degree of access to the Internet provided by the library. This statistic can also be used to produce the following composite and performance measures: average uses per workstation (when used with number of public access Internet workstation users), and public access Internet workstations in proportion to the legal service population. The library can use this statistic to compare itself to peer libraries within the state and across the nation.

Suggestions on the uses for this measure include:

- Shows extensiveness of Internet access across the state.

- May suggest patterns of Internet access (urban/rural) that may be addressed at the state level and can help pinpoint areas of the state where access is deficient due to a small number of workstations per population served.

- Useful for tracking the impact of special state and national initiatives, for example, Library Services and Technology Act (LSTA) goals, Gates Foundation, State Library connectivity initiatives.

- Useful to know when state agencies ask the State Library whether they can safely direct their clients to the local public library to access information they make available on their web sites.

- Useful to demonstrate the benefit of supporting public libraries as a way to provide this local public access to the Internet and government information.

- Useful to demonstrate public libraries' contribution to education since after school and home-schooled students can use the Internet at public libraries when the public library has sufficient numbers of public access Internet workstations to accommodate them.

- Useful when conducting needs assessments to determine public library technology needs. Helps the State Library agency set grant funding priorities.

- Can help justify funding from state government for public library technology.

SAMPLE NEWS RELEASE

Library to Request Funds for Computers

Somewhere, Mich. Last night at the City's budget session, Library Director R explained to the City Council that our local library rates far below the state's standards for **public access Internet workstations**. The average number of workstations per 1,000 people in our state is X. In our community there are only Y workstations for every 1,000 persons in the Library's service area. The Library is requesting funds over a three-year period to bring the number of Internet workstations up to the state average. By purchasing three computers a year over the next three years the Library would achieve the state average.

At the local level, public access workstation figures can assist in determining the availability of access to electronic resources and services to patrons. The State Library can use the total number of public access Internet workstations in the state's libraries as an effective way to demonstrate the libraries' commitment to providing public access, provide targeted funding to underserved areas, and as a factor for seeking additional funding. At the national level, such figures can provide a means through which to determine national estimates of access by state, region, urban/rural classifications, poverty, population of legal service area, and a number of other factors.

Number of public access Internet workstation users

Definition: Annual count of the number of users of all of the library's graphical public access workstations connected to the Internet computed from a one-week sample.

Collected by: Library collects.

Survey Period: Select a one-week sample period within a predetermined one-month period once a year. This week should be a "normal" or "representative" week where possible because the results will be used to calculate an annual figure based on the one-week sample period chosen. One week equals the number of hours the library is open over a consecutive seven-day period and may vary among libraries surveyed. Should the library wish, two sample weeks may be chosen and averaged. For further discussion see "Selecting 'Typical' Weeks to Sample" in Chapter 5.

Procedure: 1) Designate a staff member to coordinate the collection of this statistic. Key tasks include: distributing a daily tally sheet, collecting the daily tally sheet and adding each day's totals to a weekly figure, and being available to respond to data collection problems should they arise.

2) Select a one-week sample period.

3) Assign a number or designator to each public access Internet workstation whose usage is to be counted. This ensures that everyone knows which machine is being counted and later which machine has certain usage figures.

4) Select the method to be used to count the number of users of the library's public access Internet workstations depending upon local practice. Common methods used include: staff observation of workstation usage (continuous or every X minutes), tallying of registration sign up sheets, or automatic counting via computer software (e.g., Historian; see Appendix C). Librarians using the observation approach may wish to use the log sheet shown in Figure 2-3.

5) Total the number of users of all of the library's graphical public access Internet workstations connected to the Internet during each sample weeks chosen.

6) Multiply the sample users for one sample week by 52 to obtain the annual total.

Special Considerations: Do not include staff use of these resources. Count each user that uses the graphical public access Internet workstations regardless of the amount of continuous time spent on the computer. A user who uses the library's workstations three times a week would count as three users in the count. A user who uses the workstation once in the morning and again that afternoon would count as two users. A user who accesses the Internet for a continuous hour counts once. A user of a public access Internet workstation who only takes one minute to look up a stock quote on the Internet

counts once. Internet use includes all types of usage including WWW, e-mail, telnet, chat, etc.

Known reasons for inaccuracy: The study team recognizes the potential difficulty of determining whether a user on a multipurpose (CD-ROM access, word processing, etc.) workstation is using the Internet. Deriving an annual figure from a one-week sample has inherent risks for accuracy. Data collection by observation is laborious, however, and some library users may view sign-up sheets as invasive.

Analysis and Use: The number of public access Internet workstation users is used to create the performance measure: average use per public access Internet workstation. Library managers have used this statistic and measure to decide where to place newly purchased workstations, identify equipment in need of repair, or to identify underutilized workstations. Program planners have used this statistic and measure to identify branches and community areas with high workstation use to target for special programs. This statistic may be used to justify the need for additional equipment for this highly regarded service.

Suggestions from study participants on uses for this measure include:

- Demonstrating, when used in conjunction with the number of public access Internet workstations, the overall usage (or overuse, as suggested by some) of the public access Internet workstations.

- Demonstrating demand/popularity of the service.

- Justifying funding for additional public library workstations to meet demand.

- Comparing attendance, program attendance, and similar measures of numbers of users.

- Showing relative use of technology compared with traditional services.

- Comparing/evaluating libraries of similar size.

Even this basic measure of use will have a noted impact.

Maximum bandwidth of public access Internet workstations

Definition: A description of the maximum bandwidth offered on public access Internet workstations, e.g., less than 56kbps, 56kbps, 128kbps, 1.5mbps, etc.

Collected by: Library collects.

Survey Period: Measure once annually.

FIGURE 2-3   Example of a Public Access Internet Workstation Observation Usage Log

Workstation Number or Designation:		
Library:	Day:	Date:
Morning (10 am – 2 pm)		
Afternoon (2 pm – 6 pm)		
Evening (6 pm – 9 pm)		

Procedure: 1) Select a fixed date to measure the maximum bandwidth of public access Internet workstations statistic.

2) Determine what is the maximum bandwidth of Internet access offered by the library to users at the public access Internet workstations as of the fixed date. Common measures of bandwidth include: 56kbps, 128kbps, 1.544mbps. If you offer Internet access only by modem, look on the modem, the software program running the modem, or in its manual for an indication of the maximum bandwidth. If you offer Internet access via an Internet service provider (ISP) this is likely to be the source of your maximum bandwidth connection. Contact your ISP to obtain the maximum bandwidth you have purchased (or otherwise obtained). Your ISP may be another unit of local government; if so, contact that unit's system department.

3) Consider using the Public Access Internet Workstation Inventory Work Form shown in Figure 2-2 when collecting this data.

Special Considerations: The term "bandwidth" as used here differs from "speed." The speed changes depending on how many computers are on the network, time of day, types of files being loaded, etc. Bandwidth basically asks how much information could be transferred if everything was optimal. The number requested is *not* an average. This number is the maximum bandwidth offered even if it is only at one public access Internet

workstation. The bandwidth of Internet access offered to staff is not considered here. Do not add the various bandwidths of the different methods of providing access to the library users. For example, if the library has two 56kbps modems the maximum bandwidth offered is 56kbps (and not 56kbps + 56kbps = 112kbps).

Analysis and Use: The maximum bandwidth of public access Internet workstations offered by the library is a useful measure of the quality of access provided. The library cannot offer certain services or the service is ineffective if the access bandwidth is too low. Comparisons with peers and state and national norms (made possible by collecting this statistic) may result in local leverage to increase the maximum bandwidth offered by the local library.

Suggestions from study participants on uses for this measure include:

- Helps to estimate the quality of Internet access in different public library locales.
- Can be used to set grant funding priorities and justify state expenditures to improve the bandwidth.
- Indicates the adequacy of the infrastructure.
- May help in design of the web sites targeted to public library users. For example, if access to most libraries is via low bandwidth modems, then web sites targeted to these libraries will need to take the low bandwidth into account when designing web sites.

Since almost all public libraries now have Internet access, this statistic helps document a critical issue: inadequate and too slow Internet access.

Electronic Services

Number of virtual reference transactions

Definition: Annual count of the number of reference transactions using the Internet. A transaction must include a question received electronically (e.g., via e-mail, WWW form, etc.) *and* responded to electronically (e.g., via e-mail). The count excludes reference questions asked in person at the library whose answer is found using Internet resources or whose answer is sent via the Internet (i.e., via e-mail). Both request and answer must be transacted via the Internet. Count excludes phone and fax traffic unless the question-answer transaction occurs via the Internet.

Collected by: Library collects.

SAMPLE NEWS RELEASE

Library's Reference Department on the Internet

Big City, Penn. Lawrence Counter, reference librarian at the Big City Free Library, has connections. Known to the residents of Big City as <LC@BigCityLibrary.gov>, he connects people to the information they're looking for. LC used to answer most reference questions in person, for people who appeared before his desk. Now, with the prevalence of Internet, he gets at least as many questions from people who reach him via the World Wide Web or e-mail.

Pointing to his computer, LC remarks, "Last month 53% of all the reference questions I handled were *virtual reference transactions.*" And that's good, he maintains, because the library has so many resources online, waiting to be connected to the people who want them. Business people get connected to resources LC finds on Business Source Elite, one of the POWER Library databases available through Big City Library. People get connected to full-text consumer health information from a variety of sources, including Health Source Plus, another POWER Library database. What are you looking for? Chances are LC, with all his connections, can help.

Survey Period: This statistic can be surveyed in the same manner as the library surveys other reference transactions.

Procedure: 1) Designate a staff member to coordinate the collection of this statistic. Key tasks include: distributing a daily tally sheet, collecting the daily tally sheet, and adding each day's totals to a weekly figure; and, being available to respond to data collection problems should they arrive.

2) Transactions may be via e-mail, a form on a web page, etc. Virtual reference transactions may involve more than reference desk staff (e.g., web master, various reference personnel, library director, volunteers, etc.). Establish an administrative procedure to report virtual reference transaction counts from the range of different potential staff sources to a designated staff person, no matter who receives the questions or answers the reference requests.

3) Disseminate the new procedure and rationale. Several notices throughout the year may be necessary.

4) Report a virtual reference transaction as you would a face-to-face reference transaction. Thus, one e-mail request may contain several reference questions taking varying time to complete. For example, one e-mail request contained two relatively short reference questions and one reference question that took ten to fifteen minutes to answer. Count the number of questions, not the number of requests. So, in the example you would report three (3) as the number of virtual reference transactions even though there was only one request. Report counts using preestablished local library reporting periods (weekly, monthly, etc.).

Special Considerations: The count excludes reference questions asked in person at the library whose answers are found using Internet resources or whose answers are sent via the Internet (i.e., via e-mail). Both request and answer must be transacted via the Internet. Count excludes phone and fax traffic unless transaction occurs via the Internet.

The library may wish to also keep track of reference questions whose answers are found using Internet resources or whose answers are sent via the Internet (i.e., via e-mail). See in Appendix A, "Statistics and Measures Needing Further Consideration."

Analysis and Use: Libraries are making more of their services available electronically. Libraries at the local, state, and national levels are interested in tracking the development of a new and emerging library service. There is a need to better document this transition to facilitate and improve resource allocation activities. The composite measure total reference transactions combines the number of electronic reference transactions with the number of face-to-face reference questions. The total reference transactions measure more fully represents reference activity in the local library.

Number of staff hours spent servicing public service information technology

Definition: Annual count of the staff hours spent in servicing information technology in public service area computers based on a one-week sample. Information technology servicing may include installation, repair and maintenance of hardware and software. Examples include fixing printer jams, adding paper to printers and copying machines, re-booting frozen software, installing new or upgraded software or hardware, etc. Break down reports by information technology staff, paid public service staff (professional librarian, paraprofessional), volunteer, and total.

Servicing may be done by trained information technology technicians attached to library systems units, computer labs, public service units, commercial concerns under contract to the library, or personnel from other units of local government. Servicing may also be done by public service staff including professional librarians, paraprofessionals, and volunteers whose principal responsibilities involve providing services to the public. For example, most staff members of a public library's reference and circulation departments (including their volunteers) are public service staff for the purposes of this statistic. Paid public service staff include professional librarians and paraprofessionals working in public service areas. Public service information technologies may include telephone, copy machines, video equipment, fax machines, public access Internet workstations, CD-ROM players, printers, etc. Report the totals in the following categories: Information technology staff, paid public service staff total (professional librarians + paraprofessionals), volunteer, and total (information technology staff + paid public service staff total + volunteers hours).

Collected by: Library collects.

Survey Period: This statistic should be sampled at the same time as number of paid public service staff hours spent directly serving the public. This will increase the accuracy of the performance measure: Level of paid public service effort in serving information technology. Select a one-week sample interval within a selected one-month period once a year. This week should be a "normal" or "representative" one where possible because the results will be used to calculate an annual figure based on the one-week sample period chosen. One week equals the number of hours the library is open over a consecutive seven-day period and may vary across libraries surveyed. Should the library wish, two sample weeks may be chosen and averaged. For further discussion see "Selecting 'Typical' Weeks to Sample" in Chapter 5.

Procedure: 1) Designate a staff member to coordinate the collection of this statistic. Key tasks include: distributing a daily tally sheet, collecting the daily tally sheet, and adding each day's totals to a weekly figure; and, being available to respond to data collection problems should they arrive.

2) Each day during the sample period use a prepared tally sheet made available at each public service point in the library. The tally sheet should instruct the staff to count how much time they spend in five-minute increments in servicing public access information technology. In each category, add the total number of hash marks, multiply the total by five (as each hash mark represents five minutes servicing the technology), then convert the total number of minutes to an hourly figure. Consider using the daily tally sheet shown in Figure 2-4.

Information technology technicians may have other preestablished mechanisms for accounting for their time that they may use to compile their portion of this statistic.

3) Calculate the weekly and annual totals and report the information technology staff, paid public service staff, volunteer, and total staff hours spent servicing public access information technology. Consider using the work sheet shown in Figure 2-5.

Special Considerations: The intent is to capture the time spent servicing public service information technology, not administrative or staff information technology. *Note:* If you do not have information technology staff members, enter 0 in the appropriate box in Figure 2-5.

Analysis and Use: This statistic tracks the amount of time required to service publicly accessible information technology by key staff members: information

FIGURE 2-4 Staff Hours Spent Servicing Public Access Information Technology Daily Tally Sheet

Library:		Day:	Date:

Put a hash mark (/) for each 5-minute unit spent servicing public access information technology.

	Information Technology Staff	Paid Public Service Staff (professional librarians and paraprofessionals)	Volunteers
Morning (10 am – 2 pm)			
Afternoon (2 pm – 6 pm)			
Evening (6 pm – 9 pm)			
Subtotals (total number of hash marks × 5 minutes and converted to hours)			
Total (add information technology staff *and* paid public service staff *and* volunteer subtotals)			

technology staff, public service staff, and volunteers. Questions that this statistic may help answer include:

- Is too much time spent in this area?
- Are additional technical staff needed?
- Is too much time spent by paid public service staff members who have other responsibilities?
- Does this lead to a productivity deficit in other library services?
- What is the tangible contribution of volunteers in this area?
- Does longitudinal data suggest that training programs can reduce time spent in this area?

One library used these data to justify retaining a full-time technician to provide some of these services. Some libraries may find it helpful to collect additional data in this area, specifically, what was serviced. One library used these data to identify aging equipment and justify replacement. Another library used these data to document the need for network software reconfiguration and fine-tuning. Other libraries have begun volunteer programs and increased technical training for public service staff to meet this need.

Suggestions from study participants on uses for this measure include:

- Could be used to show need for technical assistance, adequate public library personnel, and continued funding for equipment.
- May help justify state appropriations for continued public library operational expenditures to support technology instead of one-time grants for equipment.
- Could be used to justify regional plans for technical assistance.
- Could justify increase in technical staff or skill upgrades.
- Could be used to develop standards and guidelines for staff and service.
- Could be used for identifying training needs/ programs.

If the amount of time is very high, it may be necessary to develop programs to assist libraries in reducing time spent servicing information technology.

Databases

Number of full-text titles available by subscription

Definition: Count of the number of full-text titles to which the library subscribes and offers to the public

FIGURE 2-5   Staff Hours Spent Servicing Public Access Information Technology Weekly Work Sheet

Library:			For Week Beginning:	
Day of Week	**Information Technology Staff Hours**	**Paid Public Service Staff Hours** (professional librarians and paraprofessionals)	**Volunteer Hours**	**Daily Hours Subtotal**
Sunday				
Monday				
Tuesday				
Wednesday				
Thursday				
Friday				
Saturday				
Weekly subtotals by staff type				
Annual Totals (multiply the weekly subtotals by 52)				

computed one time annually and reported in three categories: serial titles, other titles, and total titles. Use the same standard definition of a serial title as is presently used with the local paper-based collection. The other titles categories may include e-books, encyclopedias, indexes and abstracts, photo archives, etc. A subscription consists of a contractual agreement or license between the library and a provider to offer one or more databases for library use under certain conditions. Excluded are short-term agreements to test a product. Database access provided by consortia should be considered a subscription if the local library contributes money to the consortia for this purpose. State Library provided databases should also be considered a subscription for these purposes. To avoid double counting titles, State Library agencies and public libraries will need to develop a reporting system that adjusts the number of full-text titles when presenting statewide statistics. *Note:* Some

contractual agreements may not include monetary payment. For example, a local electronic full-text provider, like a local newspaper, may agree to allow the library to make the full text of the newspaper available at no charge to the library. Specifically excluded are the range of full-text titles available on the Internet for which there is no agreement to offer access between the provider and the library.

Collected by: Vendors partially supply. Library counts.

Survey Period: Measure once annually.

Procedure: 1) Set a fixed date to count this statistic. Note that the date may be determined by the availability of vendor provided data.

2) Request from licensed database subscription vendor(s) a current machine-readable list of full-text titles

offered in the licensed databases to which the library subscribes. Specifically, ask the vendor to count and identify the number of full-text titles offered per database; and calculate the total full-text titles from the entire host by adding up the total unique electronic full-text titles from each database(s).

State Libraries or consortia may want to supply their members with lists and counts in each category (serial titles and other titles) of full-text titles to aid local libraries compiling this statistic. But they may be limited in what they provide by what they can obtain from participating vendors.

3) Compare the licensed database lists where necessary to eliminate duplicates. If machine-readable lists of full-text serial titles can be obtained, the lists can be combined, sorted by title (word processing or database software could be used), and duplicates eliminated (by visual inspection of titles).

4) Separate the resulting list of full-text titles into two files (or lists if doing manually): full-text serial titles and other titles. Local libraries may wish to make the resulting list of electronic full-text serial titles available to the public (if they do not do so already) or combine the electronic with the paper-based serial title list so that the expanded range of serial offerings is more widely known.

5) Compute and report the totals for each category: serial titles, other titles, total titles.

Special Considerations: Exclude periodical indexes from the serial count unless local or State Library paper-based serial count practice permits. Specific items in the other titles category, for example, e-books, may well deserve their own separate category in the future. Some libraries may want to track additional categories now.

Analysis and Use: It is important for librarians, staff, and patrons to know what the library owns or has specifically obtained access to in either print or electronic format. A list of electronic full-text titles available via subscription not only enhances a library's collection, it enhances the ability of departments such as interlibrary loan and reference to better aid their users. Electronic access has dramatically expanded access to a range of useful materials for library users. This statistic begins to document the degree of expansion of electronic resource availability to justify continuation and enhancement of these services. For example, a principal use for this statistic is to add the full-text serial titles count to the existing count of paper-based serial titles to form the composite measure, total number of serial titles offered, and performance measure, percent of serial titles offered in electronic form. Both measures provide evidence to justify the importance of electronic resources and services to the local community by illustrating the greatly expanded local access to magazines, journals, and newspapers provided by the Internet.

Note: For the remaining database statistics, libraries should note that they will only receive usage reports for the database services to which they subscribe. State Library and other provided database use will not be reflected in the reports.

Number of database sessions

Definition: Count the total number of sessions (logins) initiated in the online databases to which the library subscribes.

Collected by: Vendor supplies.

Survey Period: Measure once a month.

Procedure: Request the licensed database vendor(s) to (1) count the number of started sessions in each database for a specified month; and (2) calculate the total sessions in the host by adding the number of sessions from each database.

Special Considerations: In consortial environments, multiple libraries and remote users have access to licensed database(s). In those instances, break down the number of logins to the entire host by Internet protocol (IP) address or library name and by specific time periods.

Analysis and Use: Libraries can use this statistic to assess the peak load on the licensed database system as well as to provide an estimate of the number of database users. Through aggregation, such data can provide a picture of online database usage at the state and national levels as well by such key demographic variables as urban/rural classification, region, state, and population of legal service area. Figure 2-6 provides a work sheet that can help libraries view the database usage across databases.

Number of database queries/searches

Definition: Count the total number of searches conducted in a library's subscription to online databases.

FIGURE 2-6   Work Sheet for Number of Electronic Network Sessions

	Database 1	Database 2	Database 3
Number of sessions			
Total Sessions to Host			

FIGURE 2-7   Work Sheet for Number of Electronic Network Queries/Searches

	Database 1	Database 2	Database 3
Number of searches			
Total Searches to Host			

Collected by: Vendor supplies.

Survey Period: Measure once a month.

Procedure: Request the licensed database vendor(s) to (1) count the number of searches performed in each database for a specified month; and (2) calculate total searches in the entire host by adding the total number of searches in each database together.

Special Considerations: In consortial environments, multiple libraries and remote users have access to licensed database(s). In those instances, break down the number of searches conducted in the entire host by IP address or library name.

Analysis and Use: This statistic provides libraries with an indication of which databases are most heavily used, areas of user interest, database popularity, and a level of usage detail that goes beyond an initial session. It also can provide important information for billing purposes, as some vendors charge for databases usage by searches. Figure 2-7 provides a work sheet that can assist libraries to review their online database query/search activity across databases.

Number of items examined using subscription services

Definition: Count the number of views to each host to which the library subscribes. A view is defined as the number of full-text articles/pages, abstracts, citations, and text only, text/graphics viewed. A subscription consists of a contractual agreement or license between the library and a provider to offer one or more databases for library use under certain conditions. Excluded are short-term agreements to test a product. Database access provided by consortia should be considered a subscription if the local library contributes money to the consortia for this purpose. *Note:* Some contractual agreements may not include monetary payment. For example, a local electronic full-text provider, like a local newspaper, may agree to allow the library to make the full text of the newspaper available at no charge to the library. Specifically excluded are the range of full-text titles available on the Internet for which no agreement between the provider and the library is necessary for access.

Collected by: Vendor supplies.

Survey Period: Measure once a month.

Procedure: Request the licensed database vendor(s) to (1) count the number of views in each database for:

- Full-text articles,
- Full text-pages,
- PDF articles,
- PDF pages,
- Abstracts,

FIGURE 2-8 **Work Sheet for Number of Electronic Network Views**

Type of View	Database 1	Database 2	Database 3
Number of full-text articles			
Number of full-text pages			
Number of abstracts			
Number of citations			
Number of text only			
Number of text/graphics			
Number of PDF articles			
Number of PDF pages			
Total Views to Host			

- Citations,
- Text only,
- Text and graphics; and

(2) calculate total views to the host by adding the total views in each database. Consider using the work sheet shown in Figure 2-8.

Special Considerations: Most licensed databases now offer the ability to print, e-mail, or download or save a document. Break down the total views to the host by each of these enhancements.

Analysis and Use: This statistic estimates one facet of virtual material use in a way comparable to the traditional circulation of a book measure. However, because of the tracking capabilities of the networked environment, libraries are able to receive substantial detail of material usage such as the number of documents e-mailed, printed, or otherwise used. Thus it is combined with traditional use statistics to form the composite measure total library materials use.

Specific uses for this statistic include:

- Identifying the types of viewing in which users engage through the various subscription databases;

- Describing the various services users take advantage of or make use of while using database material;
- Assisting libraries to determine user-preferred file formats and access means; and
- Informing the database billing process, as some vendors charge by the type of file downloaded or accessed.

This statistic, therefore, details the activities in which users engage with online database material. As such, it can assist libraries to tailor the database services that they provide users through their subscription services.

Appendix B provides users with a tutorial on how to import selected vendor data reports into Microsoft Excel for analysis purposes.

Virtual Visits

Number of virtual visits to networked library resources

Definition: Count visits to the library via the Internet with a breakdown by:

- Number of internal virtual visits: Visits while library users are in the library using public access Internet workstations (excludes library staff and staff workstations);
- Number of external virtual visits: Visits while library users access the library remotely (excluding the visits made by library users within the library using the public access Internet workstations); and
- Total number of virtual visits: A total count of both internal and external virtual visits.

Include a note in a comment subfield if unable to count some of the library's virtual visits.

A *visit* occurs when a user connects to a networked library resource for any length of time or purpose (regardless of the number of pages or items viewed). Examples of a networked library resource include a library OPAC or a library web page.

In the case of a user visit to a library web site a user who looks at sixteen pages and fifty-four graphic images registers one visit on the web server. Because of various web server issues and differing software this measure is an *estimate* of the visits to the web site. One definition (from the *MS Site Server* manual) of a virtual visit is: "A series of consecutive requests from a user to an Internet site. If your log file data includes referrer data, then new visits begin with referring links external to your Internet site. Regardless of whether or not you have referrer data, if a user does not make a request after a specified time period, the previous series of requests is considered to be a completed visit." Another log analysis software provider, WebTrends, defines a visit using the phrase "user session. A session of activity (all hits) for one user of a web site. A unique user is determined by IP address or domain name. By default, a user session is terminated when a user falls inactive for more than 30 minutes." An alternative approach is to assign each visitor unique authentication tags that are attached to each transaction.

Collected by: Library collects. The library's Internet service provider (ISP) may also supply some or all of the data required, if the library does not host its own web site.

Survey Period: This statistic can be surveyed continuously to be compatible with turnstile counts.

Procedure: 1) Identify all electronic sources of visits to the library. This may involve activity that takes place on more than one computer server. Some of the computer servers may be owned by the library, some may be

owned by another local government agency, ISP, or other library vendors (e.g., library OPAC provider).

2) Separate the various sources of virtual visits into staff internal, public internal, and public external. Two common approaches are using IP address or some form of authentication tagged to each transaction. Exclude internal staff from the counts for this measure where possible. In terms of external visits to the library, three common sources are: external access to the library's web page, remote logins (sessions) to non–web-based library databases, and a remotely accessible library OPAC.

3) Develop strategies for collecting the needed data from each of these sources of virtual visits. Different software may be necessary to measure each electronic source of virtual visits. In some cases, the library may calculate the virtual visits using one or more log analysis software packages. In other cases, the external owner of the computer server or service (the ISP) must provide the data. Discussions may need to be held with these service providers to obtain the needed data. In still other cases, computer monitoring software may be appropriate. A list of such software appears as Appendix C.

4) In the case of a library web page housed on a library server, identify, configure, and install appropriate log analysis software. Determine log analysis software definition that corresponds to the virtual visit definition. *Note:* All log analysis software may not track virtual visits the same way so the count obtained will necessarily be an estimate. Arrange with the server technical staff for regular (e.g., monthly) reporting of internal staff visits (for your own internal use if interested), internal library user visits at the various public access Internet workstations, external library user virtual visits, and total virtual visits (internal public visits plus external visits, excluding staff use). Run the log analysis software.

5) In the case of library web pages housed on an ISP server, identify the log analysis software that the ISP uses. Determine the definition of "visit" used by the log analysis software that corresponds to the virtual visit definition with the assistance of the ISP. Arrange with the ISP for regular (monthly) reporting of internal staff visits (for your own internal use if interested), internal library user visits at the various public access Internet workstations, external library user virtual visits, and total virtual visits (internal public visits plus external visits, excluding staff use).

6) Combine the virtual visit counts from all of the various sources of virtual visit data to obtain the three counts reported here: number of internal virtual visits, external virtual visits, total virtual visits.

Special Considerations: To use this statistic the library must offer electronic access to one or more of its resources, for example, a library web page, library OPAC, or networked CD-ROM databases that can be accessed by library users. If you do not offer such a service, do not report this statistic.

Specifically exclude staff virtual visits where possible. One approach commonly used is to identify the IP addresses of the staff workstations and have the log analysis software exclude them from the count.

The number of external virtual visits count can be combined with the annual attendance in library count of visitors to the library's physical premises to obtain a more representative composite measure: total library visits. Thus, the virtual visits from those using networked services within the library are excluded to reduce double counting. Some libraries may also wish to consider two related measures not included here:

- Number of virtual visits after hours: Using the same virtual visit definition, track visits when the library buildings are closed and not providing traditional services.
- Number of virtual library visits compared with other web services: Using the same virtual visit definition compare the library virtual visit statistic with similar figures from other web pages. For example, compare the virtual visits from the library web page to those from the local city government web page or school district web page or other community service pages.

Users of the manual may develop additional methods to extend the usefulness of these counts.

Known reasons for inaccuracy: After one user connects to the Internet, several searches could be conducted in the electronic service by several users. In some cases, for example, with Internet accessible OPAC use inside the library, several users one after the other might make use of the same established connection. In most systems, a connection is cut off after a specified time of non-use, thus solving part of the problem. The best existing method of collecting virtual visits is to use log analysis software. The log analysis software producers may define virtual visits differently. For example, does a visit end after a time-out period of thirty minutes, fifteen minutes, or some other time. The recommended time-out period is thirty minutes but a local library may have to accept the available log analysis software's definition even if it varies from the above. Indicate in a comment field the software used and definition used if the definition significantly varies.

Some libraries will find it difficult to report every virtual visit. For example, libraries may have difficulty counting the use of library OPACs because their vendors do not provide this information. Indicate in a comment field those sources of virtual visits not counted. Do not estimate virtual visits for which data are not available.

Another problem that several field test libraries faced was counting dial-up visitors when they were dynamically assigned IP addresses, as is common. Libraries with more than one modem often combine them into modem pools. Each time a dial-up visitor types something and sends it to the library's modem pool, the contact is dynamically assigned to one of the library's IP addresses. That means that when the user first contacts the library, the contact is assigned to one IP address. When the user then selects something from a library menu (e.g., the library OPAC) the user's next contact is assigned another IP address. Then when the user indicates that she wants, for example, to do a title search, that contact is assigned still another IP address. Each time a library visitor types something and sends it to the library a new IP address is assigned to the transaction. At this point, the software used to count library visitors would have counted this one visit three times rather than once, and the visit may not be completed yet! There are several software fixes in the works for this problem but as of this writing, these virtual visitors cannot be counted with any validity.

Analysis and Use: This measure is a more accurate alternative to the commonly collected statistic: hits. This statistic can be combined with other electronic statistics to produce the measures: total library visits, percent of remote library visits, and total amount of network services provided.

Suggestions for uses for this statistic by local library managers include:

- Number of external visits can show that the library is in use when not physically visited and when the library is closed.
- Another way to demonstrate, particularly to technophobes, that money spent on electronic resources and services is money well spent.
- This figure has been persuasive in demonstrating the dramatic increase in use of the library because of the use of the library's Internet-based services.

Library Users—47,000 of Them Are Virtually There

Your town, Penn. Marian Lender, Director of the County Library System, is smiling. Yes, the Library seems as busy as ever—with preschoolers in for story time, a local club meeting in the community room, every seat filled in the reading room and every computer being used for Internet access—but Marian knows it's twice as busy as it looks. For every person you see, there is at least one other you cannot see. "Last month, the number of virtual visits to the Library—visits to the Library's web site to use Library resources online—was as high as actual attendance in the Library. People visited our system libraries in person 45,000 times. But they made 47,000 virtual visits from remote locations during the same time period."

Why make a virtual visit to the Library? If I'm on the Internet, can't I find everything I need? "I hear that a lot," responds Marian. "But we offer additional resources that you won't find with an Internet subscription alone. Our Library offers the POWER Library—a collection of full-text reference databases including current and back issues of 2,000 periodical titles, an encyclopedia, reference tools for young people and an archive of over half a million historic and current news photographs." In addition, the Library's catalog is available; Library patrons can check to see if the book they want is in and then reserve it online.

The Library System's address is <http://www.CountyLibrary.org>.

• This statistic has been used as leverage to acquire additional funds for electronic services due to obvious high demand.

Local libraries may take the additional step of tracking which parts of the web site are used and where users are coming from (e.g., which search engine or which geographic area). This analysis can improve the quality of the web site, identify potential hardware/software/design problems, target collection development, and focus staff instruction. Commercially available log analysis software can provide such information.

Library without Walls

Key City, Mich. It used to be that you had to go into a building to visit the Library. But no more, as Library Director Kisha Smith explained at this week's Rotary meeting. According to statistics that the Library is now keeping for the first time, virtual visits to the Library's web site is up to about 1,000 hits a month. This increases the **total Library visits** by about one-third. Ms. Smith went on to explain that people who visit the virtual Library check on availability of materials, use the reference resources, even look up magazine, journal, and encyclopedia articles from databases made available through a grant from the state. The Library building is only open 56 hours a week, but resources on the web page are available any time. Our patrons can do all their research at home and then come in to pick up materials later. This new interest in the virtual Library reflects the interest in the community at large in electronic resources and the efficient use of time.

The number of external visits counts virtual library visitors and annual attendance in library counts physical visitors to the library. When combined these statistics form the composite measure total library visits. These measures are particularly useful as public libraries establish their virtual presence on the Internet. Many public libraries go to a great deal of labor and expense to encourage virtual visits to the library without receiving any tangible credit for virtual visits. These measures begin to assess virtual visits' contribution to library services. Over time, libraries will need to decide how to allocate resources between their virtual libraries and their physical libraries. This statistic will help by providing an indication of which location (physical or virtual) library users are using and to what degree.

Suggestions from study participants on uses for this measure include:

• May be used to show continued relevance of public library service if physical attendance figures go down.

• Helps to justify state funding for statewide database licensing and union catalogs on the web.

- May enable tracking of how this new and emerging service affects all library activity.

- Shows which libraries in which parts of the state attract virtual users. Can then analyze in conjunction with demographic data.

- Helps in development of state level information systems policy by counteracting the idea that libraries are becoming obsolete.

This is a very useful measure for showing the importance and necessity of having public libraries in a virtual environment.

Instruction

User information technology instruction
Report number of users and hours

Definition: Count of the information technology instruction of library users conducted or sponsored by the public library. Break down by the number of users instructed and the number of hours of instruction. Information technology instruction includes help in using the technology as well as assistance in using resources obtainable using information technology. Instruction may be delivered via structured, informal, or electronically delivered sessions. Structured means a lecture, public meeting, or course with a designed curriculum intended to demonstrate the use of a technology such as the Web, Internet searching, library workstation, personal computing, etc. Informal includes contacts with users by library staff of ten continuous minutes or more whose purpose might be to demonstrate the use of library workstations, introduce resources available on a popular topic or aspects of the applications available on a workstation, etc.

An electronically delivered user instruction session should be supplied or recommended by library staff. Electronic instruction might involve an Internet-based course or distance learning, a computerized learning module, or an instructional video related to use of information technology or resources obtainable using information technology. Sponsored means that the library plays some role (not limited to instruction) in the user instruction session. For example, the library might provide meeting space for a computer class taught by a local community college instructor.

Collected by: Library collects.

Survey Period: Formal user instruction should be measured continuously. Informal user instruction data collection should be keyed to reference service sampling. Select a one-week sample interval within a selected one-month period once a year. This week should be a "normal" or "representative" one where possible because the results will be used to calculate an annual figure based on the one-week sample period chosen. One week equals the number of hours the library is open over a consecutive seven-day period and may vary across libraries surveyed. Should the library wish, two sample weeks may be chosen and averaged. For further discussion see "Selecting 'Typical' Weeks to Sample" in Chapter 5.

Procedure: 1) Include only instruction in the use of information technology or resources obtainable using information technology. Examples of user instruction include use of the web, Internet searching, use of public access Internet workstations or personal computers, subject-based resources available on the Internet, social implications of information technology (e.g., filtering and the public library). Instruction may be formal, informal, or electronic.

2) Formal user instruction: Count all users attending and the length of formal, structured lectures, public meetings, or courses in the use of information technology or resources obtainable using information technology that the library offers or contracts for, or that use library facilities. A sign-up sheet may be the most appropriate technique. Consider using the tally sheet shown in Figure 2-9.

3) Informal user instruction: Count the number of users instructed and hours of informal instruction in the use of information technology or resources obtainable using information technology at various public service locations in the library (e.g., the reference desk) whose duration is ten minutes or more of continuous (rather than cumulative) user contact. Exclude ready reference and traditional reference questions using preexisting, locally developed guidelines. Note the emphasis here is on instruction, not question answering (even though in practice the distinction between the two is not always clear). Avoid double counting. Add informal user instruction to traditional reference service tally sheets or create a separate tally sheet similar to the one shown in Figure 2-10.

4) Computer-based (and other electronic) instruction: Instruction in the use of information technology or resources obtainable using information technology that is delivered electronically by the library should also be

FIGURE 2-9 Weekly Formal User Instruction Tally Sheet

Library:			Date Week Begins:	
Date	**Sponsor**	**Instruction Subject**	**Number of Users**	**Session Length** (in minutes)
			Totals:	

FIGURE 2-10 Daily Informal User Instruction in Use of Electronic Resources and Services

Library:			Day of Week/Date:	
Put a hash mark (/) for each 10-minute unit spent providing information technology training.				
	Count (using hash marks)		**List Today's Popular Instruction Topics**	
Morning (10 am – 2 pm)				
Afternoon (2 pm – 6 pm)				
Evening (6 pm – 9 pm)				
Number of users instructed (total the number of hash marks for the day)				
Number of hours of instruction (Multiply number of users trained by 10 minutes and then divide by 60 to obtain hours. Report in quarter hour increments.)				

counted even if there is little personal involvement with library staff on site. Examples might include:

- Taking a web-based course on Java computer programming,
- Enrolling in a distance learning course on e-commerce,
- Using a computerized learning module to write a resume on a personal computer at a library-supported community computer lab, or

- Using a library audio or video cassette that provides an introduction to the Internet.

Libraries should count all of these electronic instruction sessions in the use of information technology or resources obtainable using information technology.

5) Add formal, informal, and electronic user instruction activities to form a cumulative: number of users instructed and number of hours of instruction.

Special Considerations: Exclude instruction of staff here. Exclude user instruction *not* in information technology-related areas like those in the examples above.

Count users instructed whether unique or not. For example, a user asks for an instruction module on using the Internet to obtain employment. The next day the same user asks for the same instruction module again. The following day the same user asks for instruction in how to use word processing software to write her resume. Count all three instruction occasions.

Libraries encourage independent learning and avoid monitoring of information resource use where practical. Given these principles, count only those instances where a library staff member recommends or provides specific access to an information technology instruction resource. For example, a user asks a reference librarian for help in learning to use the Internet. The librarian recommends the use of a "Learning to Use the Internet" tutorial available on the Internet. Count this instance. In another case, a user at a public library's Internet access workstation independently (without recommendation of a library staff member) uses the same Internet tutorial available on the Internet. Do *not* count this instance.

Include only those informal user instruction sessions that are ten (or more) *continuous* minutes in length. Exclude cumulative cases where a series of short "double-back-and-check" informal instruction contacts that a reference staff person might have with one user total five to ten minutes (or more) during the course of a desk shift.

Count information technology instruction regardless of the media used: face-to-face, Internet, CD-ROM, video, audio, etc. A user need not be a registered library user. A single individual may attend multiple instruction sessions of the same or different types, each of which is counted. So if a single individual attended a structured introduction to the Internet session and received a fifteen-minute informal introduction to employment resources on the Internet at the reference desk the number of users instructed count would increase by two and one hour would be added to number of hours of user instruction. Electronically delivered instruction is limited to that recommended or supplied by library staff because of the difficulty of measurement or measuring without disturbing user privacy and confidentiality.

A library staff member need not be present during the instruction session. For example, a local community college might contract with the library to provide a college course (using college staff) introducing the Internet at the library. Student attendance at each class session should be counted. In another example, a local computer club holds a session at the library to introduce a new computer operating system. Count the number of attendees at the meeting in the user instruction total.

Analysis and Use: The public library is the place to go to learn about the latest information technology in a number of communities. A newly valued role for public libraries in their communities is as information technology instructor. This statistic measures public library contributions in this area. Some libraries have made instruction in the use of electronic resources and services a priority and seen explosive growth in this service area as a result. Reference units have been renamed the Reference and Instruction Department to reflect the change in function. These libraries have strongly advocated for statistics and measures to justify this shift in focus. Other libraries are beginning to offer instruction in the use of electronic resources and services and seek ways to monitor use of instruction services so that resources may be shifted as needed. Most libraries have seen noticeable increases in informal instruction in the use of electronic resources and services. This measure provides a way of accounting for this service.

Many libraries may choose to collect additional user instruction information, specifically what the subject of the instruction received was. See the suggested forms Figure 2-9 and Figure 2-10. This additional information enables local libraries to:

- Identify and correct hardware, software, and design problems so that use of electronic resources will be easier,
- Develop needed instructional materials,
- Prioritize staff instruction needs, and
- Build library collections in neglected but popular areas.

Local libraries may find that collecting this additional data to be a useful activity.

Senior State Library officials have suggested that these measures can be:

- Useful in encouraging state and local agencies to direct their clients to public library Internet instruction.
- Helpful in tracking the development of a new and emerging library service.
- Useful to a State Library agency located within a Department of Education where the meaning and

value of instructional activities may be better understood than other library activities.

- Helpful in promotion of public libraries as partners in technology education.
- A tool to provide useful briefing material for news media, educators, and legislators.
- Used to compare libraries and also related to demographic data.

This measure demonstrates the extensiveness of the educational/instruction function of public libraries.

Staff information technology instruction

Definition: Annual count of the total number of staff instructed and the number of hours of formal instruction in the management or use of information technology or resources obtainable using information technology. Report a breakdown by number of staff instructed and number of hours of staff instruction. Formal means a session, conference, workshop, instructional learning module, distance learning program, or course with a designed structure or curriculum. Examples include a preconference workshop on establishing a volunteer program to assist in the provision of Internet access, a distance education course on copyright in the digital era, or use of a computerized interactive learning module on web page design. Count computer and other electronic-based instruction along with face-to-face instruction. Staff counted includes professional, paraprofessional, and volunteer staff as well as board members. Excluded staff include janitorial and maintenance personnel.

Collected by: Library collects.

Survey Period: This statistic should be surveyed continuously throughout the year.

Procedure: 1) Designate a staff member to coordinate data collection, publicize the need to report training activities, to collect self reports, and summarize staff information technology instruction data.

2) Develop an effective plan for collecting data on all formal staff training across all library units and libraries. Some libraries find it helpful to include these activities in staff monthly activity reports. Consider using the tally sheet shown in Figure 2-11.

Note that this tally sheet asks for additional information that may be of interest to the local library beyond what needs to be reported for this recommended statistic.

3) Summarize the various staff training activities across the library(ies) and report number of staff instructed and number of hours of staff instruction totals. Report hours in quarter hour increments. For example, a instruction class lasting seventy minutes should be counted as 1.25 hours.

Special Considerations: Exclude informal staff instruction. Exclude staff instruction if *not* in information technology related areas.

Include only instruction in the use of information technology or resources obtainable using information technology. Examples of staff instruction include a class on the use of the web, a conference workshop on employment resources available on the Internet, a conference workshop on public library use of filtering software. Instruction may also be on information technology other than the Internet. Instruction may be face-to-face or electronic.

A single staff member may attend multiple instruction sessions of the same or different types, each of which is counted. For example, a single staff member attends a course on using the Internet at a local community college lasting six hours and attends a workshop on

FIGURE 2-11   Staff Instruction Tally Sheet

| *Circle one:*   Board   Professional   Paraprofessional   Volunteer | | | | |
Date	Staff Member Name	Staff Category (board, professional librarian, paraprofessional, volunteer)	Brief Description of Instruction Activity	Session Length (in minutes)

Internet resources on aging lasting one hour, and watches a one-hour video from the Public Library Association on filtering and public libraries. The number of staff instructed count would increase by three and the number of hours of staff instruction count would increase by eight. If thirty staff members from the same public library attend the same one hour preconference workshop on an information technology topic, the number of staff instructed count would increase by thirty and the number of hours of staff instruction count would increase by thirty.

Procedures may need to be developed to ensure that *all* staff report their formal information technology training on an ongoing basis.

Analysis and Use: Today's library staff require continuous instruction just to keep up with the introduction of new information technologies. This statistic begins to describe how libraries are responding to this challenge. A local library will be able to compare the number of staff it instructed and the number of hours of instruction with peer libraries and eventually state and national norms. This statistic can also be used to calculate the hours of information technology instruction per staff member performance measure. This may result in greater allocation of resources for staff instruction.

Many libraries may wish to collect additional staff instruction information, specifically who received the instruction and what the subject of the instruction received was. See the suggested form, Figure 2-11. This additional information may enable local libraries to:

- Allow department heads to have a better sense of who within their unit knows what;
- Identify those who may be left out of instruction activities;
- Identify key areas of staff training needs; and
- Increase the visibility and perceived importance of instruction.

Local libraries may find that collecting this additional data is a useful activity.

Use by a State Library: State Libraries are seeking ways to stimulate interest in information technology instruction. Continuing education for public library staff is now a legal requirement in Pennsylvania. This statistic will help libraries demonstrate that they have met the standard. Other State Libraries are considering similar requirements. This measure begins to describe the information technology instruction situation within the state and will be useful for planning for the provision of future State Library sponsored instruction sessions.

Suggestions from study participants on uses for this measure include:

- Demonstrating compliance with state and other mandated staff instruction;
- As a way to describe the information technology instruction situation within a library system, throughout a state, or across the nation;
- Assisting library systems, state library agencies, federal agencies, and professional organizations to develop, plan, and conduct instruction programs that meet the needs of the profession and library staff; and
- May enable comparison of the amount and types of instruction offered through various instruction programs so as to avoid duplication of effort.

Libraries continue to seek ways of measuring and promoting information technology instruction for public library staff.

ADDITIONAL STATISTICS USED IN CONJUNCTION WITH RECOMMENDED STATISTICS

The following statistic is not widely collected by public libraries at present. This statistic does not measure electronic resources and services. It is included here because it may be used with the electronic resources and services statistics recommended above to produce the composite and performance measures recommended in Chapter 3.

Number of Paid Public Service Staff Hours Spent Directly Serving the Public

Definition: Count of the paid public service staff hours spent directly serving the public at some service point, for example, staffing the reference or circulation desks. Staff counted includes professional librarians and paraprofessionals and the reference and circulation desks along with others. Excluded staff include janitorial and (noninformation technology) maintenance personnel. The scheduled hours of direct public service that each public service staff member provides should be added together. This statistic will be used with number of staff hours spent servicing public service information technology to form the performance measure: level of paid public service effort in servicing information technology.

Collected by: Library collects.

Survey Period: Local library chooses the same one-week period within a selected one-month period once a year as it selects for the number of staff hours spent servicing public service information technology statistic. This week should be a "normal" or "representative" one where possible because the results will be used to calculate an annual figure based on the one-week sample period chosen. One week equals the number of hours the library is open during a consecutive seven-day period and may vary across libraries surveyed. Should the library wish, two sample weeks may be chosen and averaged. For further discussion see "Selecting 'Typical' Weeks to Sample" in Chapter 5.

Procedure: 1) Select a one-week period during the survey period. If possible, select the same data collection week that the number of staff hours spent servicing public service information technology data are collected. This week should be a "normal" or "representative" public service staffing week if possible because the results will be used to calculate an annual use figure based on the one-week sample period chosen. Should the library wish, two sample weeks may be chosen and averaged.

2) Identify each of the public service points in the library and the staff serving them.

3) Determine the total number of professional librarian and paraprofessional staff hours directly devoted to serving the public. Consider using the work sheet shown in Figure 2-12.

FIGURE 2-12   Paid Public Service Staff Hours Spent Serving the Public Tally Sheet

Service Point	Reference Desk			Circulation Desk			Other Service Point		
	Professional Librarians	Para-professionals Service Staff	Total for Paid Public	Professional Librarians	Para-professionals Service Staff	Total for Paid Public	Professional Librarians	Para-professionals Service Staff	Total for Paid Public
Sunday									
Monday									
Tuesday									
Wednesday									
Thursday									
Friday									
Saturday									
Grand Totals									

3

Recommended Composite and Performance Measures

This chapter illustrates some, but not all, of the potential uses of the recommended electronic resource and services statistics described in Chapter 2. The recommended statistics can be combined, often with traditional measures such as circulation, to form composite measures. The recommended statistics can also be divided into ratios to produce performance measures. Each description of the recommended composite or performance measures contains a definition, method of calculation, and suggestions for analysis and use. Figure 3-1 summarizes the recommended composite and performance measures. Appendix A contains additional statistics and measures that local libraries may want to consider.

As a library considers the recommended measures, the most important question to ask about composite and performance measures may relate to credibility. Do you or key local stakeholders think you are combining or relating apples and oranges? If so, the credibility of the composite or performance measure is challenged and its utility may be reduced.

RECOMMENDED MEASURES

Public Access Internet Workstations in Proportion to the Legal Service Area Population

Definition: The ratio of population of the library's legal service area to number of public access Internet work-

stations. For example, XYZ public library provides one public access Internet workstation per 3,000 legal service population. The population of the legal service area is commonly collected as part of annual surveys. The measure counts the number of people in the geographical area for which a public library has been established to offer services, and from which (or on behalf of which) the library derives income, plus any areas served under contract for which the library is the primary service provider. The measure uses the latest U.S. Census Bureau data and is often supplied to public libraries by the State Library.

Calculation: The population of the library's legal service area is divided by the number of public access Internet workstations in the library.

$$\text{One public access Internet workstation in proportion to some amount of the legal service area population} = \frac{\text{Legal service area population}}{\text{Number of public access Internet workstations}}$$

Analysis and Use: The North Carolina Public Library Directors Association has already established the following guideline:

FIGURE 3-1   Composite and Performance Measures

Measure	Definition
Public access Internet workstations in proportion to the legal service area population	The ratio of the legal service area population to number of public access Internet workstations., e.g., XYZ library provides 1 public access Internet workstation per 3,000 legal service population.
Average annual use per public access Internet workstation	The ratio of the number of public access Internet workstation users to the number of public access Internet workstations.
Total reference activity	Combine traditional measures of reference service with electronic measures.
Percentage of virtual reference transactions to total reference questions	Percentage of number of virtual reference transactions to total reference questions (both traditional and virtual).
User information technology instruction as percentage of total reference activity	The number of users instructed in information technology as a percentage of total reference activity.
Level of paid public service effort in servicing information technology	Percentage of paid public service staff time spent servicing information technology during a sample period.
Total library materials use	Combines the circulation and use figures for all of the paper, multimedia, and electronic collections that the public library owns or to which it provides access.
Percentage of electronic materials use of total library materials use	Compares electronic materials use in the form of number of items examined using subscription services with the total library materials use.
Total number of serial titles offered	Count of paper-based serial titles added to number of full-text serial titles available by subscription.
Percentage of serial titles offered in electronic form	Compares number of unique electronic full-text serial titles available by subscription with the total number of serial titles offered.
Total library visits	Physical attendance at the library and number of virtual visits combined into one total.
Percentage of remote library visits	The percentage of external virtual visits to total library visits (virtual plus physical library visits).
Percentage of legal service area population receiving information technology instruction	The percentage of the legal service area population receiving information technology instruction annually from the public library.
Hours of formal information technology instruction per staff member	The average number of hours of formal information technology instruction a public library staff member receives per year.

"Each library facility has at least one computer workstation for every 2,500 people in its designated service area," <http://ils.unc.edu/daliel/NCPLDA/guidelines/>.

Other population breakdowns can be used (as the numerator of the ratio) including population served (i.e., public access Internet workstation per some amount of population served) and registered borrowers (i.e., public access Internet workstation per some amount of the library's registered borrowers) to create alternative local performance measures.

Average Annual Use per Public Access Internet Workstation

Definition: The ratio of the number of public access Internet workstation users to the number of public access Internet workstations.

Calculation: Divide the number of public access Internet workstation users by the number of public access Internet workstations.

$$
\text{Average annual use per workstation} = \frac{\text{Number of public access Internet workstation users}}{\text{Number of public access Internet workstations}}
$$

Analysis and Use: The use of any individual workstation can be compared to the average use per workstation. If the use is unusually low, the workstation can be checked for problems or relocated. If the workstation use is high, additional workstations can be added. A similar study can be done at an outlet level. It is possible to compare the average use per workstation figure with peer, state, and national averages as well.

Total Reference Activity

Definition: The combination of traditional measures of reference service with electronic statistics. Traditional reference counts include face-to-face reference questions, telephone and fax reference counts, mediated online searches. Electronic statistics include number

of virtual reference transactions and user information technology instruction in ratio to number of users instructed.

Calculation: Add counts for traditional reference transactions to counts for electronic reference transactions. Add face-to-face reference questions and ready reference counts, telephone and fax reference counts, mediated online searches plus the number of virtual reference transactions and number of users instructed in information technology.

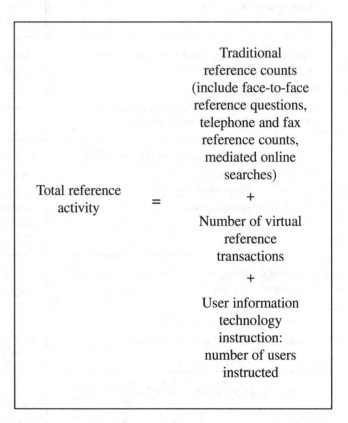

$$
\text{Total reference activity} = \begin{array}{c} \text{Traditional reference counts (include face-to-face reference questions, telephone and fax reference counts, mediated online searches)} \\ + \\ \text{Number of virtual reference transactions} \\ + \\ \text{User information technology instruction: number of users instructed} \end{array}
$$

Analysis and Use: This composite measure more fully accounts for reference activities within the public library. In particular, this measure addresses fluctuations in face-to-face reference service with the introduction of various Internet-based services.

Percentage of Virtual Reference Transactions to Total Reference Questions

Definition: Percentage of virtual reference transactions to total reference questions (traditional reference questions plus the number of virtual reference transactions).

Calculation: Divide the number of virtual reference transactions by the total number of reference questions (including virtual reference transactions, face-to-face reference questions, telephone and fax reference questions) and multiply the result times 100. For example, a public library has 100 virtual reference transactions of a total reference question count (traditional and virtual) of 10,000. 100 divided by 10,000 equals .01 times 100 equals 1%. Thus virtual reference transactions represented 1% of the library's total reference questions.

$$\text{Percentage of virtual reference to total reference questions} = \frac{\text{Number of virtual reference transactions}}{\text{Number of reference questions} + \text{Number of virtual reference transactions}} \times 100$$

Analysis and Use: This performance measure provides an indicator of comparison between virtual and the total number of reference questions asked. If this service grows as anticipated, this measure will track the transition and offer an indicator to assist decision makers in reallocating resources.

User Information Technology Instruction as Percentage of Total Reference Activity

Definition: The number of users instructed in information technology as a percentage of total reference activity.

Calculation: Divide the user information technology instruction: Number of users instructed by the total reference activity and then multiply by 100.

$$\text{User information technology instruction as percentage of total reference activity} = \frac{\text{User information technology instruction: number of users instructed}}{\text{Total reference activity}} \times 100$$

Analysis and Use: This is a quick way of comparing information technology user instruction activities to reference service overall. This figure can be compared over time, among peer libraries, to statewide and national data.

Level of Paid Public Service Effort in Servicing Information Technology

Definition: The percentage of public service staff time that is spent serving the public on the reference desk servicing information technology during a sample period.

Calculation: This performance measure requires the collection of an additional statistic: number of paid public service staff hours spent directly serving the public. For a description of this new statistic, see Chapter 2. Both statistics should be sampled at the same time. Divide number of public service staff hours spent servicing information technology by the number of paid public service staff hours spent directly serving the public and then multiply by 100.

$$\text{Level of paid public service effort in servicing information technology} = \frac{\text{Number of staff hours spent servicing information technology by paid public service staff (professional librarian, paraprofessional)}}{\text{Number of paid public service staff hours spent directly serving the public (professional and paraprofessional only)}} \times 100$$

Local libraries may also wish to collect the additional performance measure that adds volunteer contributions:

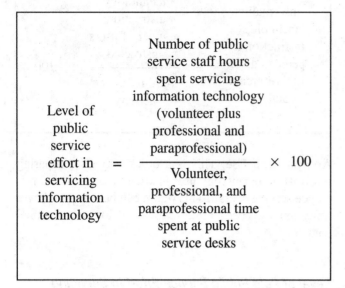

$$\text{Level of public service effort in servicing information technology} = \frac{\text{Number of public service staff hours spent servicing information technology (volunteer plus professional and paraprofessional)}}{\text{Volunteer, professional, and paraprofessional time spent at public service desks}} \times 100$$

The local library could also look at the volunteer contribution overall:

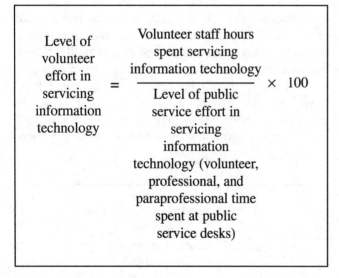

$$\text{Level of volunteer effort in servicing information technology} = \frac{\text{Volunteer staff hours spent servicing information technology}}{\text{Level of public service effort in servicing information technology (volunteer, professional, and paraprofessional time spent at public service desks)}} \times 100$$

Analysis and Use: This measure is an estimate of paid public service staff time spent in servicing information technology. This measure may suggest the need to reassign or retrain staff or develop a volunteer program so that expensive staff time is spent on other duties, or the need to hire trained staff to handle the servicing of information technology. A local library can compare itself with peer libraries and state and national averages as well.

Total Library Materials Use

Definition: This composite measure combines the circulation and use figures for all of the paper, multimedia, and electronic collections that the public library owns or to which it provides access. Combine the traditional annual total circulation count (including adult and juvenile book, serial, audio, film, and video materials circulated and renewed), and interlibrary loan items borrowed that circulate to users (exclude items checked out to another library). Then add counts from annualized samples of in-house book, periodical, manuscript and other collection use if they are normally reported on the State Library's annual survey. Include counts of any electronic media circulated including computer software and e-books. Then add number of items examined using subscription services.

Calculation: Collect traditional and electronic statistics as outlined above and total.

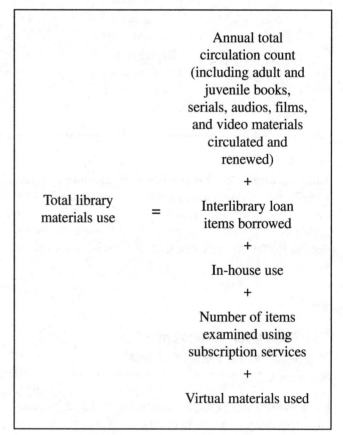

$$\text{Total library materials use} = \begin{array}{c}\text{Annual total circulation count (including adult and juvenile books, serials, audios, films, and video materials circulated and renewed)}\\ +\\ \text{Interlibrary loan items borrowed}\\ +\\ \text{In-house use}\\ +\\ \text{Number of items examined using subscription services}\\ +\\ \text{Virtual materials used}\end{array}$$

Analysis and Use: This composite measure more fully represents the number of library materials used by public library users annually. In some cases, the measure more accurately portrays the impact of a decline in use in one collection while other collections remain constant or increase. Specifically, this figure may address the concern some public libraries expressed: Is public library circulation declining or simply changing?

SAMPLE NEWS RELEASE

Library Adopts New Annual Report Format

According to Library Board President Y, the R Public Library will be using new formulas to account for library use in this year's annual report. While the library used to report circulation of books and other materials only, it will now add use of **electronic materials** (that is, materials found on the Internet) as part of circulation. Library Director P explains: "More and more people, especially kids, prefer finding information on the Internet to use of more traditional books and magazines." On paper, it looks like our library is less busy because circulation of traditional materials is down a bit. However, the fact is that we're busier than ever before and counting the use of electronic materials will help us give a better picture of the true use of the library. The fact is our circulation is one-third higher when we count the **percentage of electronic materials use of total library materials use.**

Percentage of Electronic Materials Use of Total Library Materials Use

Definition: This performance measure compares electronic materials use in the form of number of items examined using subscription services with the total library materials use.

Calculation: Divide the annual number of items examined using subscription services by the total library materials use and then multiply by 100.

$$
\text{Percentage of electronic materials use of total library materials use} = \frac{\text{Number of items examined using subscription services}}{\text{Total library materials use}} \times 100
$$

Analysis and Use: One approach to resource allocation is to assign funds based on collection use. This provides one estimate of the licensed database collection use compared with overall collections use. Similar performance measures could be calculated for other portions of the library's collections. See the limitations to this measure discussed under "Total Library Materials Use," above.

Total Number of Serial Titles Offered

Definition: This composite measure adds the traditional count of (paper-based) serial titles to the recommended statistic: number of unique electronic full-text serial titles available by subscription.

Calculation: Add the traditional number of (paper-based) serial titles to the number of unique electronic full-text serial titles available by subscription.

$$
\text{Total number of serial titles offered} = \begin{array}{c} \text{Number of (paper-based) serial titles} \\ + \\ \text{Number of electronic full-text serial titles available by subscription} \end{array}
$$

Analysis and Use: This composite measure allows local libraries to begin to describe the impact of new electronic serials, including electronic magazines and newspapers, in their collection using tangible evidence.

Percentage of Serial Titles Offered in Electronic Form

Definition: This performance measure compares number of unique electronic full-text serial titles available by subscription with the total number of serial titles offered.

Calculation: Divide the number of unique electronic full-text serial titles available by subscription by the total number of serial titles offered and then multiply by 100.

$$
\begin{array}{l}
\text{Percentage} \\
\text{of serial} \\
\text{titles} \\
\text{offered in} \\
\text{electronic} \\
\text{form}
\end{array}
=
\dfrac{\begin{array}{c}\text{Number of unique}\\ \text{electronic}\\ \text{full-text serial}\\ \text{titles available by}\\ \text{subscription}\end{array}}{\begin{array}{c}\text{Total number of}\\ \text{serial titles offered}\end{array}}
\times 100
$$

Local libraries with modest paper-based collections of serials may also want to calculate the following performance measure: Percentage of increase of serial access as the result of electronic access.

$$
\begin{array}{l}
\text{Percentage} \\
\text{of increase} \\
\text{of serial} \\
\text{access as} \\
\text{the result of} \\
\text{electronic} \\
\text{access}
\end{array}
=
\dfrac{\begin{array}{c}\text{Number of}\\ \text{unique}\\ \text{electronic}\\ \text{full-text serial}\\ \text{titles available}\\ \text{by subscription}\end{array}}{\begin{array}{c}\text{Number of}\\ \text{(paper-based)}\\ \text{serial titles}\end{array}}
\times 100
$$

Analysis and Use: This performance measure allows a local library to describe the impact of the introduction of electronic resources, such as licensed databases, on the library's ability to provide such popular materials as newspapers, magazines, reference sources, and other serials to the public. The impact may be more dramatic in small to medium-sized libraries when the percentage of increase of serial access as the result of electronic access performance measure is calculated.

Total Library Visits

Definition: The combination of the traditional annual attendance in library count and number of external virtual visits into one total. Annual attendance in library is a traditional count often defined as the total number of persons entering the library including persons attending activities, meetings, and those requiring no staff services.

The number of external virtual visits includes only those who access the library's Internet services remotely.

Calculation: Add the library's count of total number of physical visits (the traditional annual attendance in library count typically made using a turnstile count or a sample) to the number of external virtual visits to networked library resources.

$$
\begin{array}{l}
\text{Total library} \\
\text{visits}
\end{array}
=
\begin{array}{c}
\text{Number of}\\ \text{external virtual visits}\\ +\\ \text{Annual attendance}\\ \text{in library}
\end{array}
$$

Analysis and Use: This library use figure more fully represents the number of visitors to the library when the library maintains a presence on the Internet. The figure may help account for shifts in the number of physical visitors to the library as a result of the introduction of a virtual library on the Internet.

Percentage of Remote Library Visits

Definition: The percentage of external virtual visits to total library visits (number of external virtual plus physical library visits).

Calculation: Divide the number of external virtual visits by the total library visits and then multiply by 100. For example, if a public library had 1,000 external virtual visits and 9,000 physical visits for a total visit composite measure of 10,000. 1,000 external virtual visits divided by 10,000 physical plus external virtual visits equals .10 times 100 equals 10%. Thus, at this public library virtual visits accounted for 10% of the total visits to the library.

$$
\begin{array}{l}
\text{Percentage} \\
\text{of remote} \\
\text{library} \\
\text{visits}
\end{array}
=
\dfrac{\begin{array}{c}\text{Number of external}\\ \text{virtual visits}\end{array}}{\text{Total library visits}}
\times 100
$$

The local library may also wish to calculate another proportion of external virtual to physical library visits.

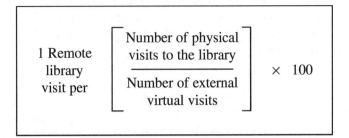

$$\text{1 Remote library visit per} = \left[\frac{\text{Number of physical visits to the library}}{\text{Number of external virtual visits}} \right] \times 100$$

For example, the library's turnstile count was 3,500 and there were 100 external virtual visits. There was one virtual visit for every 35 physical visits to the library.

Analysis and Use: This is a quick estimate comparing the remote virtual with physical visits to the public library and a partial indicator of the importance of each.

Percentage of Legal Service Area Population Receiving Information Technology Instruction

Definition: The percentage of the legal service area population receiving information technology instruction annually from the public library. The population of the legal service area is commonly collected as part of annual surveys. The measure counts the number of people in the geographical area for which a public library has been established to offer services, and from which (or on behalf of which) the library derives income, plus any areas served under contract for which the library is the primary service provider. The measure uses the latest U.S. Census Bureau data and is often supplied to public libraries by the State Library.

Calculation: Divide User information technology instruction: number of users instructed by the legal service area population and then multiply by 100.

$$\text{Percentage of legal service area population receiving information technology instruction} = \frac{\text{User information technology instruction: number of users instructed}}{\text{Legal service area population}} \times 100$$

Analysis and Use: The rapid introduction of new information technology has created the need to educate local community members to be technically literate, to be eligible for newly available jobs, or to simply retain existing employment. The public library in many communities is the place to receive information technology instruction. This performance measure provides an indication of the public library's contribution to the community in the information technology instruction area.

Local libraries may wish to consider several additional performance measures: percent of population served receiving information technology instruction or percent of registered borrowers receiving information technology instruction.

Hours of Formal Information Technology Instruction per Staff Member

Definition: The average number of hours of formal information technology instruction a public library staff member receives per year. Formal means a session, conference, workshop, instructional learning module, distance learning program, or course with a designed structure or curriculum intended to demonstrate the use of information technology or resources obtainable using information technology. Staff counted includes professional librarians, paraprofessional, and volunteer staff as well as board members. Excluded staff include janitorial and maintenance personnel.

Calculation: Divide the annual number of hours of formal information technology staff instruction by the number of public library staff.

$$\text{Hours of formal information technology instruction per staff member} = \frac{\text{Number of hours of formal staff information technology instruction}}{\text{Number of staff (professional librarians, paraprofessionals, volunteers, board members)}}$$

Analysis and Use: This performance measure offers one estimate of information technology instruction received by staff. This figure can be compared over time, among peer libraries, with statewide and national averages to describe the degree to which the library provides for staff information technology instruction.

RECOMMENDED STATISTICS REPORT FORM

Figure 3-2 presents a report form identifying all of the recommended statistics, the recommended composite and performance measures, and the traditional statistics necessary to calculate all of the measures recommended in this chapter.

FIGURE 3-2 Electronic Measures Report Form

Recommended Statistics	Results
Number of paid public service staff hours spent directly serving the public	Professional librarians:
	Paraprofessionals:
	Total:
Number of public access Internet workstations	
Number of public access Internet workstation users	
Maximum bandwidth of public access Internet workstations	
Number of virtual reference transactions	
Number of staff hours spent servicing public service information technology	Information technology staff:
	Paid public service staff:
	Volunteers:
	Total:
Number of full-text titles available by subscription	
Number of database sessions	
Number of database queries/searches	
Number of items examined using subscription services	
Number of virtual visits to networked library resources	Internal visits:
	External visits:
	Total:
Comment (if unable to count some virtual visits):	

Recommended Composite and Performance Measures	Results
User information technology instruction	Number of users instructed:
	Number of hours of instruction:
Staff information technology instruction	Number of staff instructed:
	Number of hours of staff instruction:
Public access Internet workstations in proportion to the legal service area population	
Average annual use per public access Internet workstation	
Total reference activity	
Percentage of virtual reference transactions to total reference questions	
Level of paid public service effort in servicing information technology	
Total library materials use	
Percentage of electronic materials use of total library materials use	
Total number of serial titles offered	
Percentage of serial titles offered in electronic form	
Total library visits	
Percentage of remote library visits	
Percentage of legal service area population receiving information technology instruction	
Hours of formal information technology instruction per staff member	
Traditional Statistics Used	
Population of legal service area	
Number of reference questions	
Number of persons (physically) visiting the library	
Total circulation	
Number of (paper-based) serial titles	

4

User Assessment

This chapter presents an approach to conducting a basic user assessment of the library's electronic resources and services using a questionnaire and focus group interviews. The statistics and measures presented in Chapters 2 and 3 begin to describe the library's electronic resources and services and their use. But missing from the description are:

- Who are the users of the library's electronic resources and services?

- What electronic resources and services are used, how, and why?

- To what degree are the users of the library's electronic resources and services satisfied? Why are users dissatisfied?

- What effects have these services had on library users' lives?

- What improvements should be made in the provision of electronic resources and services?

- What new electronic resources and services should be offered?

The user assessment suggested in this chapter helps complete the tool kit necessary to fully describe usefulness of the library's electronic resources and services.

A user assessment complements, deepens, and broadens the results obtained using the statistics and measures introduced in Chapters 2 and 3:

- **Complements**: Initial findings and interpretations suggested by the data from the recommended statistics and measures can be cross-checked by asking library users for their views. Survey and focus group interview results may enable you to better understand the results from the statistics and measures recommended earlier.

- **Deepens**: The recommended statistics and measures by themselves offer a basic description of *what* are the library's electronic resources, services, and their use. The user assessment can suggest *why* these resources and services matter to library users. Comments from library users may put a "human face" on impersonal numeric data, revealing the *why* behind the *what*. A survey and focus group interview can also reveal the impact of use of electronic resources and services on library users.

- **Broadens**: In addition to assessing current use of the library's resources and services and their value, users may also be asked to suggest future resources and services the library might offer. The use of open-ended questions in surveys and focus group interviews encourages the reporting of the unexpected ideas and issues not previously addressed by library managers.

Library users are central to the present and future use of the library's electronic resources and services. Obtaining user views is commonsensical and can assist librarians to better develop and deploy existing and new services.

RECOMMENDED APPROACH

This chapter provides templates for two types of user assessment: a survey questionnaire and a focus group interview. The questionnaire and interview cover four basic areas:

- Background information on the participant (e.g., name, address, etc.);
- A user assessment of present satisfaction/dissatisfaction with existing library electronic resources and services;
- Determination of key issues and needed improvements from the user perspective; and
- Recommendations for new electronic resources and services in the future.

A standard approach is to conduct a survey and additional focus group interview once during the year. At each focus group interview, the facilitator hands out a one-page questionnaire to be completed by the participants while they wait for the interview to begin. The library may decide to use these two types of assessment differently depending on local circumstances, for example, to:

- Conduct the focus group without using the questionnaire;
- Use the questionnaire without the focus group;
- Conduct one-on-one interviews rather than group interviews (with or without the questionnaire) either face-to-face, by telephone, or even via chat room or e-mail;
- Create a computer or web-based version of the questionnaire; or
- Some combination of the above.

Figure 4-1 describes a sample survey containing a *menu* of potential questions. The templates provided can be adapted for use with any of these options.

SURVEY/QUESTIONNAIRE TEMPLATE

Designing and administering a survey questionnaire and interpreting its results can be quite sophisticated. See Moran (1985), Fink (1995), Salant and Dillman (1994),

Babbie (1990), McClure and Lopata (1996, 55-76), and Walter (1992, 65-69) for additional guidance. But the basics are accessible to any librarian and the use of surveys is common in public libraries. The results you obtain will provide clues to understanding the use of the library's electronic resources and services rather than truth certain. Key tasks can be divided into planning, administering, analyzing, and reporting.

Questionnaire Planning

There are a number of tasks to complete when planning a survey:

- **Establish a timeline**, for example,

    Clarify survey objectives,

    Decide how to administer the survey,

    Choose appropriate questions,

    Identify target group(s) for survey and select a representative sample,

    Determine costs and budget,

    Assign, inform, and involve staff,

    Pretest,

    Prepare final questionnaire, print, and copy it,

    Distribute the survey,

    Collect data, send reminders if appropriate,

    Analyze data,

    Prepare reports,

    Present findings.

- **Define the library's objectives for the survey**: What purpose does the survey achieve? Why is each question asked? Who will be informed of the results of each question? Fishing expeditions, with no particular purpose in mind, often yield poor results.

- **Decide how the library will administer the survey**: For example, will the library use a survey in conjunction with focus group interviews? Will the library make a survey available for self-administration at public access workstations? Should the library conduct a survey at a relevant group event (e.g., an Internet user group meeting at the library) or conduct a mail survey, telephone survey, web-based survey, etc.?

- **Obtain any needed administrative permissions**: In some cases governing board permission may be necessary.

FIGURE 4-1   Library Electronic Resources and Services: Tell Us What You Think Survey
[Note: Libraries should substitute their information and examples throughout the form.]

Thank you for volunteering to complete this survey. *Note:* you do not have to complete this survey and you may choose not to answer any of the questions below for any reason. All responses are confidential which means that your name will not be associated with any responses you make here. This questionnaire will be destroyed immediately after the library's analysis of these surveys is complete. Once again, thank you for participating. We value your input.

A. Background Information

Name: _____ E-mail: _____ Phone: _____

Address: _____

1) What is your age (Circle one)?

   [14 or under]   [15-22]   [23-34]   [35-54]   [55-64]   [65 or more]

2) What is your gender (Circle one)?

   [Male]   [Female]

3) Do you have a current XYZ library card (Circle one)?

   [Yes]   [No]

4) What was the highest level of education you completed (Circle one)?

   [Graduate Degree]   [Bachelor Degree]   [Some college]   [High school diploma]   [Some high school]

5) How long have you used computers (Circle one)?

   [Less than 1 year]   [1-2 years]   [3-5 years]   [6 years or more]

6) How would you rate your Internet skills (Circle one)?

   [Excellent]   [Very good]   [Good]   [Fair]   [Poor]   [Have never used]   [Don't know]

7) Do you regularly access the Internet from your home or office (Circle one)?

   [Yes]   [No]

B. Internet Use in the Library

8) How often did you use the Internet at the library in the last month (Circle one)?

   [Almost daily]   [Once a week]   [1-2 times]   [Not at all]

9) Is the library's workstation the principal way you access the Internet (Circle one)?

   [Yes]   [No]

10) The library has adequate Internet access to meet my information needs (Circle one):

   [Strongly agree]   [Agree]   [No opinion]   [Disagree]   [Strongly disagree]

11) Check all that you did when you used the library's Internet workstation during the past month:

   __ Accessed information databases (e.g.,)   __ Obtained information via web sites   __ Played games
   __ Sent or received e-mail   __ Distance learning   __ Joined chat rooms
   __ Read posts from listservs or news groups __ Searched or applied for a job   __ Purchase a product
   __ Paid bills or handled personal finances   __ Read news, weather, or stock reports

   Other: _____

12) How would you rate our Internet services or a specific Internet service within the library in terms of:

	Excellent	Very Good	Good	Fair	Poor	Can't Rate
Overall experience						
Value of library service						
Access to the equipment						
Response time						
Ease of use						
Finding what you want						
Knowledge of library staff						
Courtesy of library staff						

Any comments or suggestions to improve the web site?

C. Remote Internet Use via the Library Web Site

13) How often have you used the library's web site from outside the library in the last month (Circle one)?

[Have not used]   [1-2 times]   [4-5 times]   [10-11 times]   [12+ times]

14) Check all the resources you accessed from the library's web site when you used it outside of the library during the past month?

__ Accessed information databases (e.g.,)   __ Distance learning   __ Checked library hours
__ Read news, weather, or stock reports   __ Searched or applied for a job   __ Asked a reference question
__ Obtained other information via web sites   __ Purchased a product or service

Other: _____

15) How useful did you find the content of the library's web site (Circle one)?

[Very useful]   [Somewhat useful]   [Adequate]   [Somewhat useless]   [Not helpful]

16) How easy was it to find information on the library's web site (Circle one)?

[Very easy]   [Easy]   [Average]   [Hard]   [Very hard]

17) How would you rate the library's web site in terms of:

	Excellent	Very Good	Good	Fair	Poor
Overall experience					
Value of library service					
Ease of use					
Finding what you want					

Any comments or suggestions regarding the library's web site?

(continued)

18) How do you compare the library's web site with others (Circle one)?

[Much better]   [Somewhat better]   [About the same]   [Somewhat worse]   [Much worse]

19) How likely would you be to recommend the library's web site to a friend (Circle one)?

[Very likely]   [Somewhat likely]   [Might or might not]   [Somewhat unlikely]   [Very unlikely]

20) How has using the library's Internet service changed or made a difference in your life? Please comment:

D. New Services

21) What level of priority should the following potential services receive at our library?

[1-highest priority]   [2-very important]   [3-a priority]   [4-not of interest]   [5-do not do]

__ More and/or better computers for public use
__ More online full-text journal articles (accessible from the library, home, or office)
__ Ability to place a hold on library materials (e.g., a book) from home or office
__ Online renewals
__ Home delivery of books, journal articles, etc.
__ Personally ordering via the Internet copies of articles not owned by the library for office or home delivery
__ Direct link from electronic citations to the library's holdings
__ More instruction on using the library's electronic resources and services
__ Electronic information kiosk at the local shopping center

22) If you could recommend one thing the library should do to improve its electronic services, what would it be?

- **Choose appropriate questions**: Figure 4-1 offers a menu of questions from which to select ones appropriate to the local library setting. *Note:* The questions in Figure 4-1 are suggested but not recommended like the statistics and measures in Chapters 2 and 3. If using the questionnaire with focus groups, aim for no more than one page of questions. Avoid asking questions just because the answers would be nice to know. Less is definitely more if you hope to have high returns. Surveys will gain in utility if repeated over time. Try to include questions that can be reused.

- **Identify target population and sample size**: The questionnaire in Figure 4-1 is targeted to teenage and adult users of the library's electronic resources and services. A library could also survey community members who do not presently use the library's electronic resources and services. A questionnaire to survey children's views might be prepared. But the need for data from this special population must be balanced by the special care necessary when surveying this group. See Walter (1992, 65-69) for an introduction to basic considerations when surveying children. If you are using the survey in conjunction with focus group or individual interviews, give every focus group participant a questionnaire. If you are using the questionnaire by itself, there are specific rules for determining an appropriate sample size that can be found in Babbie (1990) and Fink (1995).

- **Determine the costs and a budget**: How much is the library willing to spend in obtaining a library user's views? Common costs to consider are personnel, copying, and postage (for a mail survey) costs.

- **Assign, inform, and involve staff regarding the survey**: Hold meetings to obtain the input of library staff on a range of inputs from question selection and survey administration to ways to improve the survey process.

- **Pretest the questionnaire**: This step is easy to ignore but generally fatal if you fail to do so. Pick a small group similar in composition to the target group. The pretest group should read and complete the survey. In addition, the pretest group should provide feedback on the survey itself including readability, ease of comprehension, question clarity and lack of ambiguity, typographical errors, layout, and flow difficulties. Note how long on average it takes pretesters to complete the questionnaire. Is it too long? Staff that administer the questionnaire may have additional useful insights to offer.

Use the feedback from the pretest to create the final version of the questionnaire. Make certain that the questionnaire is easy to read and well organized with clear instructions.

Questionnaire Administration

If you are using the questionnaire by itself, a cover letter (or opening screen on a web page) may be appropriate. Mention such items as the purpose and importance of the survey, the need for a response, deadline (if appropriate), mechanics of completing and returning the questionnaire, etc. Include an appropriate statement about the voluntary nature of the survey and confidentiality of survey responses (see sample text in Figure 4-1).

Count the number of questionnaires distributed. Distribute the questionnaire during a "normal" period free of unusual events or activities that might bias the results. Collect the responses. A good response rate if you are using the questionnaire by itself is 50 to 70 percent. The response rate is a percentage calculated by dividing the count of usable questionnaires you received by the count of the total number of questionnaires distributed and then multiplying by 100. In the case of a mail survey, one or more reminders to those who are being surveyed may be necessary.

Data Analysis and Reporting

Data should be analyzed systematically and reported promptly. Some pointers to keep in mind when analyzing the data include:

- Develop a plan for how the results of each question will be analyzed, used, and reported when you select each question, not when the results are compiled.

- Keep in mind that the results you obtain are likely to provide clues or suggestions of what is going on rather than valid, reliable, and conclusive answers.

- Statistical, database, and spreadsheet software is available for analysis; spreadsheet software may be adequate.

- Ignore as unusable incomplete or blank answers. Ignore multiple responses to a question designed to have only one response. Never assume that you know what a user means.

- Calculate response rates for each question of the survey. The response rate is a percentage calculated by dividing the count of usable individual question responses you received by the count of the total number of questionnaires distributed and then multiplying by 100. A response rate for a question that is significantly lower than the average response rate may make the results suspect.

- Where appropriate, for example, question 2 in Figure 4-1, count the number of responses for each option, the total number of responses and then calculate a percentage choosing each option. For example, say 200 people answered question 2; 74 indicated that they were female; 126 checked that they were male. When presenting your summary of the findings you might report: 2) What is your gender? Male (126) 63% Female (74) 37%.

- Users' written comments in response to a question (often written in the margin) may be important. Prepare a summary of these comments for each question as appropriate.

Refer to the sources mentioned above for additional advice on analyzing the data.

Report the results of the electronic resources and services questionnaire. Remember to:

- Report your results promptly. Good data, supplied after a decision is made, have no value.

- Report the results to any staff who were involved in data collection. This way, seeking to involve staff in future surveys becomes much easier.

- Make use of graphics and figures to summarize findings where appropriate.

- Consider providing a summary report of the findings to those who participated in the survey. A report of the survey finding may provide an incentive to participate.

You might want to consider:

- Combining the results from the questionnaire with the results of the focus group interviews (if done) and the results from the statistics and measures used from Chapters 2 and 3. Be sure to indicate the source of the results used in any report. For example, "Questionnaire results suggest that . . .'"

- Using a survey respondent's comment to summarize, highlight, explain, or enrich a much longer discussion or presentation of numerical data in a report.

A plan for distribution of the results (who should receive what results in what form), developed when initially planning for the questionnaire, pays dividends now.

FOCUS GROUP INTERVIEW TEMPLATE

A focus group interview consists of a small group (5-9 people) that share their views about a predetermined topic in response to questions from a facilitator (see Figure 4-2). Sessions can vary in length; common are sessions from thirty to ninety minutes long. The sessions are often recorded or one (or more) notetakers are present. Focus group interviews, like other qualitative approaches, differ in intent from the quantitative approaches represented in Chapters 2 and 3 and partially in the questionnaire. Krueger (1994, 87) briefly summarizes the difference:

> It is important to keep in mind that the intent of focus groups is not to infer but understand, not to generalize but to determine the range, and not to make statements about the population but to provide insights about how people perceive a situation.

Designing and administering a focus group interview and interpreting its results can be quite sophisticated. See Glitz (1997), Hutton and Walters (1988), Krueger (1994), Morgan (1993), Stewart and Sharcasani (1990), and Walter (1992, 62-65) for additional guidance. But the basics are accessible to any librarian and the use of focus group interviews is common in public libraries. Key tasks can be divided into planning, administering, analyzing, and reporting.

Focus Group Interview Planning

There are a number of tasks to complete when planning for focus group interviews:

- **Establish a timeline**, for example,

  Clarify survey objectives,

  Decide how the library will administer the focus groups,

Choose appropriate questions and draft an interview script,

Select staff to assist with the focus group interviews,

Select appropriate focus group members, number of groups to interview,

Make arrangements for the interview setting,

Prepare a budget if appropriate,

Pretest script with a test group,

Prepare final focus group script and adjust group membership as appropriate,

Conduct the focus groups,

Analyze the data, and

Prepare reports.

- **Define your objectives for the focus group interview**: What does the library want to learn from these focus group interviews? What purpose does the focus group achieve? Why is each question asked? Who will be informed of each question's results?

- **Decide how the library will administer the focus group interviews**: Will you include a questionnaire? What time of year will the interviews be conducted?

- **Obtain any needed administrative permissions**: In some cases governing board permission may be necessary.

- **Choose appropriate questions**: Figure 4-2 contains a menu of suggested questions from which to select ones appropriate to the local library setting. *Note:* The questions in Figure 4-2 are suggested but not recommended like the statistics and measures in Chapters 2 and 3. Aim for around five to seven questions or key issues depending on the length of time planned for the interview.

- **Select staff to assist with the focus group interviews**: Key staff needed include a facilitator and one or more notetakers. The facilitator conducts the focus group interview following a script similar to the one in Figure 4-2. The facilitator also takes notes but may not be able to keep up with the flow of ideas and jot notes at the same time. The notetakers attend the interview and take notes either of the whole session or by attending to a certain range of comments based on a work form. A sample Staff Participant Reaction Work Sheet is shown in Figure 4-3. Often the interview is taped (with the permission of the participants) and additional staff may be needed to transcribe the data into written text from the recording. The written notes prepared by the notetakers or the transcription of the taped interview is the data that are analyzed and reported.

- **Identify the target population**: The scripted questions in Figure 4-2 are targeted to teenage and adult users of the library's electronic resources and services. A library could also interview community members who do not presently use the library's electronic resources and services. A focus group interview script to assess children's views might also be prepared. But the need for data from this special population must be balanced by the special care necessary when interviewing this group. See Walter (1992, 62-65) for an introduction to basic considerations when interviewing children.

- **Identify sample size**: How many focus groups are necessary to affect the necessary data? The general rule for determining the number of focus groups needed is to continue running them until no new information is generated. In practice, Krueger (1994, 88) suggests scheduling four and reevaluating after three. Keep in mind the intent of these interviews is to understand the users' perspective, not generalize to the entire population of users of electronic resources and services at your library.

- **Pick the members of each focus group session wisely**:
  - Choose group members who are articulate, comfortable with each other, and will not hesitate to share their viewpoint; and, taken as a whole, represent the diverse range of viewpoints on the library's electronic resources and services.
  - Krueger (1994, 17) notes that the size of the group is determined by two principal factors: "It must be small enough for everyone to have opportunity to share insights and yet large enough to provide diversity of perceptions."
  - The researcher bias here is to pick people you know or who think like you, ignoring the range of other types of users within the community. Often it is best to involve a group of public service staff members in the selection process in the hopes of capturing the range of viewpoints needed.
  - Avoid putting friends, classmates, or family members in the same group to avoid preexisting hierarchies or patterns of communication.
  - Possible groupings might be around age (e.g., teens, seniors), typical time of day (e.g., Thursday morning Internet users), interest (e.g., business users), skill level, or convenience (five library users were available to meet).
  - The library may find it appropriate to prepare a letter of invitation covering purpose of the interview, importance to the library, date and time of the interview, and voluntary nature of participation.
  - Prepare a session membership list indicating the names of each participant.

- **Make arrangements for the interview setting**: Choose a quiet, well-lit space with a table large enough to accommodate the group. Cookies and light refreshments may be offered and may encourage the reluctant to participate. Select the dates for the group interviews; if the space needs to be booked in advance, do so.

- **Determine the costs and a budget**: How much is the library willing to spend in obtaining library users' views? The costs to conduct focus group interviews are generally minimal, often limited to personnel, copying costs, and refreshment costs. Nonetheless, be certain that resources are available to support this effort.

- **Pretest the focus group script and make necessary adjustments**: Choose members like those you intend to interview. This will enable the facilitator to become familiar with the script and test the questions and process in advance. Include the results of the interview in the final report if appropriate.

Review the script in preparation for conducting the next focus group interviews.

Focus Group Administration

Figure 4-2 offers a focus group interview script template similar to the one needed to begin focus group interviews. After the session it may be appropriate to send a written thank you to each participant. Perhaps the most tedious task, yet the most important, is the preparation of the notes from each focus group session. Taped transcriptions take the longest but may be the most useful. Often the detailed notes taken by designated notetakers, which include key verbatim quotes from interview participants, are adequate. In other cases, listening for the key issues is more important than trying to capture everything that is said. A one-page Staff Participant Reaction Work Sheet similar to the one shown in Figure 4-3 may be used as necessary.

FIGURE 4-2   Focus Group Interview Script

PREPARATION FOR SESSION

Arrive at the site 10 minutes before the session is scheduled to start. Upon arrival, check to be sure chairs are arranged around the table, refreshments are delivered, etc. Bring tape recorder, tapes, and batteries, place the recorder in the center of the table, and test to see that it is working properly. Bring copies of the session membership list, questionnaires, and extra pencils. When each participant arrives check the name off against the session membership list and hand the person a copy of the questionnaire. Instruct them to fill out the questionnaire and return it to you at the end of the session. Invite them to take refreshments if they like. Arrange for chalk and blackboard should you plan to have the group rank responses to questions 2, 4, and 5.

BEGIN THE SESSION

Give the group a chance to talk together for a few minutes and finish the questionnaire after all have arrived in order to let them begin to feel comfortable with one another. After about five minutes, if they aren't seated around the table, ask them to do so and then say something like the following:

I would like to begin this focus group on the library's electronic resources and services now. Welcome, and thank you for attending. Your comments today will help all of us at the library better understand how you are using these electronic resources and services, what you value, what needs to be improved, and what resources and services we should consider adding.

These sessions are being taped in order to gain the fullest information from the comments you make. The tapes will be transcribed and listened to or read only in strict confidentiality. Your comments will be transcribed only as those made by "person 1," "person 2," etc. As soon as we have finished using your comments, the recording will be erased. Again, this information will be used only by those involved in this evaluation in order to study and improve the library's electronic resources and services. Your participation in this survey is voluntary. You may choose not to answer any of the questions asked for any reason. Once again, thank you for participating. We value your input.

Introduce any additional staff and explain their role (e.g., as notetakers). Then continue with the following:

The purpose of this survey session is to find out about your use of the library's electronic resources and services. The interview consists of several questions designed to give you a chance to describe various library experiences you may have had while here at the library or when you accessed the library's web site. Please feel free to speak at any point; however, I ask that only one person speak at a time in order that all comments can be heard. There are no "right" or "wrong" answers to these questions and it is likely that the group will have a range of different answers to the questions asked. The goal of this process is simply to gather honest responses from a variety of library users in order to evaluate our electronic resources and services.

You were asked to fill out a questionnaire when you arrived. I will collect it at the end of the session. Don't worry, there will be additional time at the end of our session to finish writing your answers. Again, there are no "right" or "wrong" answers. Just respond to each question as honestly and clearly as you can. Feel free to write in the margins or on the back of the questionnaire if you wish to respond more fully to any question.

Question 1: How do you use the Internet?

Let's start with each person giving his or her name and briefly describing the most interesting recent use of the Internet.

Turn on the tape recorder, identify yourself by giving your name, and a recent interesting use of the Internet, and proceed around the table until all have done the same. [In addition to the usage information gained, it is a good idea to begin with a question all can readily answer to make people comfortable with talking in the group.]

Probe: Does anyone use the Internet for other purposes?

If there is no response, prompt with any of the following. Do you like to:

- Access information databases (e.g.,)
- Obtain information via web sites
- Send or receive e-mail
- Participate in distance learning
- Read posts from discussion or news groups
- Search or apply for a job
- Join chat rooms
- Pay bills or handle personal finances
- Play games
- Purchase a product or service
- Read news, weather, or stock reports

Prompt until you sense that most major uses have been identified.

Probe: How often did you use the Internet from the library or via the library's web page last month?

Note the skill levels of the various participants.

Question 2: What do you like best about the electronic resources and services the library provides? Why?

Note: It might be useful to write the suggestions down on a blackboard so that they can be ranked by the group when all of the suggestions are made.

If there is no response, prompt with any of the following. How do you like:

- Access to the equipment

  Probe: Is the library the principal place you use the Internet?

- Value of library service
- Response time
- Ease of use
- Finding what you want
- Knowledge of library staff
- Courtesy and helpfulness of the library staff

Prompt until you sense that most major responses have been identified.

Probe: [If the list is not too long] How would you rank in importance the list of what you like best that the group compiled? [*Note:* This may take more time than you wish to allocate.]

Question 3: *What do you think about the library's web site?*

If no response, prompt with, Do you like the site's

- Ease of use
- Use of graphics
- Organization of the web site
- Information and links to useful sources

Prompt until you sense that most major responses have been identified.

Probe: How does the library's site compare with other sites you regularly use?

Probe: How often did you use the library's web site last month?

Probe: What could be done to improve the library's web site?

Question 4: *What should the library do to improve the existing electronic resources and services it offers?*

Note: It might be useful to write the suggestions down on a blackboard so that they can be ranked by the group when all of the suggestions are made.

If no response, prompt with:

- Additional databases.

    Probe: Which ones or which subjects?

- Training on certain topics.

    Probe: Which topics?

- More services via the Internet.

    Probe: Which ones?

Prompt until you sense that most major responses have been identified.

Probe: [If the list is not too long] How would you rank in importance the list of suggested improvements the group just suggested? [*Note:* This may take more time than you wish to allocate.]

Question 5: *What new electronic resources and services should the library offer?*

If no response, prompt with:

- More and/or better computers for public use
- More online full-text journal articles (accessible from your home)
- Place a hold on library materials (e.g., a book) from home
- Home delivery of books, journal articles, etc.
- Personally ordering via the Internet copies of articles not owned by the library for office or home delivery
- Direct link from electronic citations to library's holdings
- More instruction on using library resources
- Electronic information kiosk at the local shopping center

Prompt until you sense that most major responses have been identified.

Probe: [If the list is not too long] How would you rank in importance the list of new electronic resources and services that the group compiled? [*Note:* This may take more time than you wish to allocate.]

Question 6: *Can you think of specific ways that using the library's electronic resources and services have had an impact or made a difference to you?*

If no response, prompt with, Some library users have told us that they were able to:

- Find lost friends via the Internet
- Plan better vacations
- Find a job or prepare for a job interview
- Take or complete college courses

Prompt until you sense that most major responses have been identified.

Question 7: *Is there anything anyone would like to add regarding the library's electronic resources and services before we wrap this session up?*

WRAP-UP

Turn off the recorder and conclude by saying:

Thank you for your responses and your time. Your answers will be very helpful to us in evaluating the electronic resources and services we currently provide and the new services we may offer in the future. Please return your completed questionnaires to me now. If you need additional time I will wait.

Be sure to label recorder tapes or discs with the date, facilitator's name, and time of the interview session. Be sure to complete the Staff Participant Reaction Work Sheet.

FIGURE 4-3   Staff Participant Reaction Work Sheet

This work sheet should be completed immediately after each focus group session by the facilitator and any notetakers. It is designed to capture your principal reactions and views of the session.

1) What was the most surprising comment that was made?

2) How did this group differ from typical users of the library's electronic resources and services?

3) What needs to be changed/revised before the next session?

4) What did the group like best about the existing library electronic resources and services?

5) What are the principal improvements to the library's electronic resources and services recommended by the group?

6) What new services did the group recommend?

7) Any comments you want to make about the process?

Focus Group Data Analysis and Reporting

Data should be analyzed systematically and reported promptly. Some pointers to keep in mind when analyzing the data include:

- Develop a plan for how the results of each question will be analyzed, used, and reported when you select each question, not when the results are compiled.

- The results you obtain are likely to provide clues or suggestions of what is going on rather than valid, reliable, and conclusive answers.

- Conduct the analysis of the focus group session as soon as possible after the session concludes while the memories of facilitator and notetaker(s) are fresh.

- One way of preparing an analysis of focus group interviews is to create a session report for each interview. A session report uses the questions asked as major headers, identifies major themes discussed in response to each question under sub-headers, summarizes each theme, and is sure to include key quotes made by session participants as evidence.

- Session reports for each interview are combined to form the basis for the final focus group interview report.

- Report your results promptly. Good data, supplied after a decision has been reached, have limited value.

- Make use of graphics and figures to summarize findings where appropriate.

- Do not forget to report the results to any staff involved in data collection. Involving staff in future surveys becomes much easier if they receive prompt reports on their efforts.

- Focus group data should be combined with data from the questionnaire, if used, and data from the statistics and measures in Chapters 2 and 3 when creating a final report on the public library's electronic resources and services.

A plan for distribution of the results (who should receive what results in what form), developed when initially planning for the focus group interviews, pays dividends now.

Conducting a user assessment using survey and focus group interviews will complement, deepen, and broaden the library's evaluation of its electronic resources and services. Key findings will include:

- An assessment of present user satisfaction/ dissatisfaction with existing library electronic resources and services;

- Determination of key issues and needed improvements from the user's perspective; and

- Recommendations for new electronic resources and services in the future.

As such, a user assessment is an integral part of any evaluation of the library's electronic resources and services.

5

Managing Data Collection and Use

Chapter 5 reviews the basic issues and techniques necessary to collect and use the statistics and measures of electronic resources and services introduced in earlier chapters. The emphasis is on review, as this work supplements the advice offered by earlier output measure manuals for public libraries (Van House et al., 1987), children (Walter, 1992), young adults (Walter, 1995) and school media programs (Bradburn, 1999). All of the manuals recognize the importance of embedding the recommended measures in the library's planning process and considering at the start the full measurement life cycle, from choosing measures, staffing, and scheduling, to data collection, analysis, and reporting and use.

MEASUREMENT AND
THE PLANNING PROCESS

The measures recommended here, like the earlier output measures, gain in value when integrated into existing local library planning efforts. For example, the recommended measures might be integrated with any of the approaches offered in recent planning manuals by Adcock (1999), Himmel and Wilson (1998), Mason (1999), Mayo and Nelson (1999), and Nelson, Altman, and Mayo (2000).

The strength of the adoption of the recommended measures is that the same definitions and procedures for collection are available to all libraries that use these standardized measures. This makes comparison with other libraries possible. The weakness of recommending measures for use across the nation is that initially these measures can appear foreign or externally imposed from outside the local library. A key outcome from embedding the recommended measures in a local library's planning process is that the local library staff makes these measures their own. Key questions like:

- What do the measures mean and mean for us locally?

- How do these measures assist the library to achieve its goals and objectives?

- Who should collect what measures and when?

- Who cares locally about the results and why? and

- How can the measure help (or hurt) library interests?

get answered in a way that matters to local library staff and key community stakeholders. The once foreign measures become the local library staff's own. Anyone who has had the experience in using any measure in isolation versus using the measure as an integrated part of a planning process will never wish to live in isolation again.

The need for good communication is important throughout the process and critical during the planning and data collection phases. Communication patterns begun during the planning phase endure throughout the measurement life cycle. Mechanisms for communicating with all relevant staff should be established. Special attention should be given to communicating with others who may be affected by or interested in your decisions. Ask widely for input related to key decisions such as selection of measures, scheduling, anticipated problems, and potential uses for the results. Pay attention to negative feedback especially during the planning stage. Problems ignored or missed during the planning period may surface during later phases of the measurement cycle and adversely affect the success of measurement.

CHOOSING MEASURES

The central question for the local library remains: is the value of the measure's results worth the effort necessary to obtain them? The results of the recommended measures can add value in several ways:

- **Compare**: The results tell how well the library is doing compared with past performance or peers, best practices in the profession, or compared with the library's objectives.

- **Diagnose**: The results can diagnose or document problems, better define issues, or suggest solutions and ways to work smarter.

- **Inform**: The results can improve the library's image and inform and shape opinion among library staff, key stakeholders, and the community. Can you write a headline using the likely results from the proposed measure?

- **Justify**: The results can be used to justify new staff, resource allocations, or budget requests by, for example, proving use. The old "trust me, trust me" may no longer be enough when it comes to electronic resources and services.

- **Orient**: The results describe and summarize what is going on at present in the library and may redefine the meaning of success. Some libraries will find that these measures help the organization migrate away from traditional ways of managing and providing service.

- **Reward**: The results can identify organizational units and programs deserving of commendation and reward.

- **Sanction**: The results can be used to meet state standards and administrative regulations.

Hidden within the question of the value of the results is the question of value to whom? For example, library planners now know that neglecting to motivate those who will collect the data creates uncommitted record-keepers who may compromise a measure's results. When deciding on a measure's value, look along the measurement life cycle because each step in the process and each person involved can affect the results. Is there value for those who plan, collect, analyze, report, and otherwise handle or use the measure and its results? If there is limited value, can or should inducements be offered to match the effort required?

Choosing measures of electronic resources and services may also be driven by very pragmatic concerns. On the one hand, many of the recommended measures gain in value when compared over time, so the sooner data collection starts, the better. But on the other hand, local conditions, for example, limited staff, may make adoption of all of the recommended measures problematic. Some of the measures require the assistance of external partners, the Internet service provider, OPAC vendor, or licensed database providers. These partners may not be able to deliver the data to the library in the usable form needed at present. Finally, some of the measures, for example, number of virtual visits, may need technically trained personnel using log analysis software to produce necessary data. For these and other local reasons, a library may well decide to introduce only some of the recommended measures initially. The rest of the relevant measures may be introduced at a later date. Figure 5-1 is a guide to the level of effort required for the recommended measures and statistics.

Figure 5-1 identifies the recommended composite or performance measure in the far left column. The next column identifies all of the statistics necessary to generate the measure, both the traditional and the new electronic resources and services statistics. The next three columns identify the source(s) of the data needed. If a "Y" appears in the "Existing" column it means the data is generally collected as part of existing state or national library surveys. If a "Y" appears in the "Tally" column it means the library must conduct a count to obtain the needed results. If a "Y" appears in the "Software" column it means that software may be used to obtain the required data. If a "Y" appears in the "External partner" column it means the library may need to coordinate data collection efforts with an external partner (e.g., Internet service provider [ISP] or licensed database vendor) to obtain needed data. A "Y" in the Sample column means that the data need not be collected continuously. Instead

FIGURE 5-1   Level of Effort Required for Recommended Composite and Performance Measures

Composite or Performance Measure	Statistics Used	Data Source				Sample	Time Elapse	Level of Effort
		Existing	Tally	Software	External Partner			
Public access Internet workstations in proportion to the legal service area population	Number of public access Internet workstations	Y	Y				One time count	L
	Legal service area population							
Average annual use per public access Internet workstation	Number of public access Internet workstations		Y	Maybe for use count		Y	1 week	M
	Number of public access Internet workstation users							
Total reference activity	Traditional reference count	Y	Y	Maybe (computer lab use)		Y	1 week	H
	Number of virtual reference transactions							
	Number of users instructed in information technology							
Percentage of virtual reference transactions to total reference questions	Number of virtual reference transactions	Y	Y	Maybe (computer lab)		Y	1 week	H
	Total reference questions							
Level of paid public service effort in servicing information technology	Public service hours spent servicing information technology		Y			Y	1 week	M

Y = Yes   L = Low effort   M = Medium effort   H = High effort

Composite or Performance Measure	Statistics Used	Data Source				Sample	Time Elapse	Level of Effort
		Existing	Tally	Software	External Partner			
Level of paid public service effort in servicing information technology (continued)	Number of paid public service staff hours spent directly serving the public		Y			Y	1 week	M
Total library materials use	Total circulation count	Y	Y		Y database vendor			M
	Number of electronic full-text items examined							
Percentage of electronic materials use of total library materials use	Number of electronic items examined		Y		Y database vendor			M
	Total library materials use							
Total number of serial titles offered	Number of serial titles	Y	Y		Y database vendor			M
	Number of unique electronic full-text serial titles available by subscription							
Percentage of serial titles offered in electronic form	Number of unique electronic full-text serial titles available by subscription	Y	Y		Y database vendor			M
	Total number of serial titles offered							
Total library visits	Number of external virtual visits	Y	Y	Y log analysis	Maybe ISP			M

Y = Yes   L = Low effort   M = Medium effort   H = High effort

(continued)

Composite or Performance Measure	Statistics Used	Data Source				Sample	Time Elapse	Level of Effort
		Existing	Tally	Software	External Partner			
Total library visits (continued)	Attendance in library	Y	Y	Y log analysis	Maybe ISP			M
Percentage of remote library visits	Number of external virtual visits	Y	Y	Y log analysis	Maybe ISP			M
	Total library visits							
Percentage of legal service area population receiving information technology instruction	Number of users instructed in information technology	Y	Y	Maybe (computer lab)		Y	1 week	M
	Legal service area population							
Hours of formal information technology instruction per staff member	Number of hours of formal information technology instruction	Y	Y	Maybe (computer lab)		Y	1 week	M
	Number of staff							
	Number of users instructed							

Y = Yes   L = Low effort   M = Medium effort   H = High effort

refer to the "Time Elapse" column for the recommended sample period length. The "Level of Effort" column is an estimate of the effort a library may have to make to obtain the necessary data. Figure 5-2 provides similar information for the recommended *statistics*.

HOW TRUSTWORTHY CAN OR SHOULD THE RESULTS BE?

The need for valid and reliable results that library managers can trust is as great in the digital era as in the past. When output measures were first introduced, the notion of formal evaluation was less pervasive. Library managers tended more toward an all-or-nothing approach to assessing value: either the results were trustworthy or not. Today library managers are far more adept at finding utility in results that may be less valid, reliable, or comparable than they would have accepted in the past. In the digital era, the goal remains results you can trust. More flexibility, however, may be needed as we start the process of measuring electronic resources and services.

A valid measure fully measures what it intends to measure. For example, a recommended measure is number of virtual visits to the library. The intent is to mea-

FIGURE 5-2   Level of Effort Required for Recommended Statistics

Recommended Statistic	Data Source				Sample	Time Elapse	Level of Effort
	Existing	Tally	Software	External Partner			
Number of public access Internet workstations		Y					L
Number of public access Internet workstation users		Y			Y	1 week	M
Maximum speed of public access Internet workstations		Y					L
Number of virtual reference transactions		Y			Y	1 week	L
Number of staff hours spent servicing public service information technology	Y	Y			Y	Y	M-H
Number of full-text titles available by subscription				Y			L-M
Number of database sessions				Y	Y	monthly	L-M
Number of database queries/ searches				Y			L-M
Number of items examined using subscription services				Y			L-M
Number of virtual visits to networked library resources		Y	Y	Maybe			M-H
User information technology instruction		Y	Maybe (computer lab, computer base training)		Y partial	1 week	M
Staff information technology instruction		Y					L

Y = Yes   L = Low effort   M = Medium effort   H = High effort

sure all of the occasions users access library resources made available over the Internet (like web pages and OPACs). All of the libraries conducting the pretest of this measure obtained what they thought were useful results. But several of the libraries found it impossible to obtain data on the virtual use of their dial-up OPACs. The libraries did not know a way to count these data via a software counter and the libraries' OPAC vendors did not supply this information to the libraries. Consequently, for those libraries the measure is not valid because they did not count a substantial portion of their virtual visits. Yet all of the libraries involved thought that this measure was useful, particularly if there was provision for a comment line to indicate what portion of their virtual visits was missing. What if some popular new Internet technology occurs but the number of visits cannot be measured? Should the library not introduce the popular information technology to the community because measurement of it is not valid? Should the recommended measure be rejected because it is not completely valid? The consensus was that as we start the process of measuring electronic resources and services some data were better than no data. All felt that over time a mechanism would be found to add in the missing data. The measure, although not valid in every case, should still be useful.

A reliable measure is one that everyone counts the same thing, the same way, every time. Results from the pretest of the recommended measure: number of users instructed in information technology, prompted the study team to question its reliability. The initial procedures stated that informal user instruction sessions should be fifteen minutes or more. One participating library interpreted the duration requirement to mean that a library staff member must have fifteen *continuous* minutes of contact with a library user to be counted. This library liked the measure but had a low count. Another library reading the same procedures interpreted them to mean that fifteen minutes of *cumulative* user contact was sufficient. So that the common reference practice of starting the user and subsequently checking back with them and troubleshooting would count if the cumulative total was fifteen minutes. This library's count was high. But the reliability of the measure was low due to ambiguous procedures allowing libraries to count differently. Subsequently, the measure's procedures were improved to take this reliability problem into account.

New measures may need a shakedown period, and pretesting may not catch all of the reliability problems. Anticipating the impact of future practice and technology on any recommended measure makes achieving reliability over time even more difficult. Library measurers of electronic resources and services must pay extra attention to definitions and procedures they develop or use to ensure high reliability.

The advice given by earlier output measure manuals still applies even though the recommended measures are for a digital era:

- Everyone involved in the measurement life cycle from planning, data collection, analysis, presentation, to decision making and use can affect data. Clarifying the measures' meaning, procedures, and uses with all relevant staff pays dividends later.

- This manual cannot anticipate the future, but working together, particularly with peer libraries and your State Library on standardized definitions and procedures, will increase a measure's validity and reliability over time.

- Variations in the measurement processes at the local library, like "fine-tuning" this manual's procedures, affects comparability at the peer, state, and national levels.

- At minimum, local decisions about data collection should be recorded by the data coordinator (see below) and followed consistently by everyone involved in data collection and during every cycle of data collection.

Achieving trustworthy results is a never ending work-in-progress requiring good planning, good communication, and good supervision. Basic knowledge of statistics can also help; for greater detail see standard statistics texts such as Babbie (1990) and Hefner (1998).

STAFFING

The quality of the data collected and its successful use depend directly on the coordination, skill, and interest of the library personnel and key stakeholders involved even though the recommended measures are for a digital era.

Appoint a Data Coordinator

Most libraries staffed by more than one person appoint one person to be the data coordinator during the measurement process. The data coordinator plans and manages data collection and analysis including the following specific responsibilities:

- Planning, establishing a data collection team, and scheduling data collection,

- Adapting or designing data collection methods and forms suitable to the local situation,

- Communicating clearly who does what, how, and why to each team member,

- Instructing library administrators and data collectors in their roles and responsibilities,

- Coordinating collection of data from external partners such as an Internet service provider and licensed database and OPAC vendors,

- Troubleshooting, answering questions, and solving problems,
- Analyzing and reporting the data,
- Managing quality control and uniformity in data collection and analysis, documenting problems, issues, and resolutions for future data collection efforts, and
- Instructing key stakeholders in appropriate interpretation and use of the measures' results.

Most libraries find it helpful to have a single point of contact that offers consistent and authoritative answers and problem resolution.

Data Collectors

The data collectors are at the heart of the measurement process yet they often receive inadequate attention. In some cases, regular library staff members collect the data as part of their job responsibilities. In other cases, volunteers collect some or all of the required data. These data collectors need to know the answers to several basic questions:

- What measures will be used, what do they mean, what data are necessary?
- Who will collect the data?
- When will the data be collected?
- How will the data be collected and what will be expected of each participating data collector?
- What should the public be told about the measurement process and why the library is engaged in the process?
- When will the results be reported to the data collectors?
- How will the results be used?
- What will be the consequences of the reported results for the data collectors and for the library?

Data collection often represents an addition to the normal workload and a disruption to the normal status quo. Library administrators oftentimes try to reduce other staff responsibilities while data collection is in process. The data coordinator and other key administrators need to be sensitive to the data collector's concerns; they should consider ways to motivate, and all should be prepared for the unexpected.

INSTRUCTION

Data collection and use are not new to most libraries internationally but measurement of electronic resources and services is a new focus. Instruction may be necessary in a range of areas including:

- The meaning and significance of the recommended measures for the library,
- Data collection procedures, particularly those that are new and involve computer software, for example, the use of log analysis software to compile the number of virtual visits.
- Data analysis possibilities and procedures,
- Working with ISPs or licensed database vendors to obtain data, and,
- Interpreting and presenting the results to key library administrators and community stakeholders such as library boards, local funders, community opinion makers, and the media.

The quality of the data and its successful use will depend on the skills and knowledge of the library staff and key community stakeholders. Library staff and community members may not possess all of the knowledge and skill needed to successfully interpret the recommended measures. Instruction may well be needed.

Examples of the type of instruction that may be necessary at the local library include:

- Meetings conducted by the data coordinator for the persons doing data collection. These sessions would encourage participants to raise questions and concerns early in the process.
- Formal instruction sessions, perhaps done on a regional or statewide basis, in specialized data collection techniques such as log analysis and using software to collect data for various measures.
- Workshops on ways to obtain data from external library partners such as Internet service providers, licensed database services, and OPAC vendors.
- Actual pretests of data collection instruments where staff collect data, discuss the experience, and make adjustments.
- Regional or statewide sessions on effective data analysis and presentation using data from the recommended measures.
- Briefings for key local officials on the measurement effort to prepare decision makers to understand and act on the results.

These and other instruction efforts can ensure that the measurement process is as easy as possible and the results are of the highest quality possible.

SCHEDULING

The measurement process for the recommended measures, particularly when done for the first time, is likely to take longer than anticipated. Be sure to budget extra time for unanticipated problems. The data coordinator will need to schedule time to:

- **Organize for data collection**: This phase of the process always takes longer than estimated. It includes developing an action plan and master schedule, establishing roles, responsibilities, lines of communication, written forms and local procedures, and recruiting volunteers, etc.
- **Pretest collection of statistics selected**: A pretest may well be needed particularly if measures are being collected for the first time. In a library system, a small pretest in one or more branches can save a great deal of headache before implemented systemwide.
- **Choose an appropriate time**: Select a collection time and sample period (when appropriate) to collect the recommended measures chosen.
- **Decide which measures to collect together and which to collect separately**.
- **Coordinate with other annual survey activities**: Coordinate the collection of the recommended measures with other data collection activities such as annual federal/state annual surveys and the Public Library Data Survey.
- **Schedule data collection tasks**: Determine who does what, when, how, and using what forms.
- **Arrange for external data reporting**: Arrange for the reporting of data from external partners (when required) so that usable data arrive in a timely fashion.
- **Analyze the data**: It is easy to underestimate the time required to analyze this data, particularly the first time.
- **Prepare reports**: Allow time for preparing reports and press releases and presenting results in various forums including for library staff and data collectors, library boards and funders, key local officials, and the media.

Keep in mind when developing schedules for the various key tasks that the measurement process is cyclical, often following an annual schedule. Plans and schedules developed now should be reusable the next year or the next time measurement is done if they are properly documented.

Timing

Timing is especially important when scheduling key events in the measurement cycle for the recommended measures:

- Decide when to begin data collection,
- Determine the optimal time period during which results would be most useful,
- Avoid data collection during previously scheduled or known major or unusual events or holidays,
- Coordinate efforts with the arrival or departure of key staff or governing officials, and
- Obtain needed data from external partners, i.e., ISPs, database vendors, etc.

The good news is that creating the schedule for the first annual cycle of measurement is the toughest. Subsequent years are much easier. Most field test participants plan to coordinate the data collection and use of the recommended measures with existing annual surveys because these in turn work well with budget and fiscal calendars, the school year, and library calendar of major events.

DATA COLLECTION

This manual will make data collection for networked statistics and measures easier and yield results with good validity and reliability that are more valid and reliable. The results may be compared over time and among peers. Central to this effort is the use of measures with clear definitions and easy-to-use procedures that everyone can use in the same fashion every time. Many of the issues and problems that data coordinators and collectors are likely to face have been identified and discussed in previous output manuals (see in particular, Van House et al., 1987, chapter 3). So these issues will not be discussed here. Instead, some brief general guidelines will be offered and three potential areas of concern will be highlighted.

General Guidelines

The following data collection guidelines review and supplement those offered by Van House et al. (1987, 15):

- **Follow the definitions and procedures listed in the manual**: To be useful and comparable everyone needs to be counting the same thing every time. Deviation from the procedures outlined here may make the results unreliable and noncomplete.

- **Be as consistent as possible**: The goal is for every data collector to count the same things the same way this time and in the future in order for the data to be reliable and comparable. Local procedures should be written so that future data collectors can follow the same guidelines.

- **Provide all data collectors with instruction and ready access to local guidance**: Instruction can increase motivation and ensure uniform collection. Should a problem arise during data collection, the collector should have rapid access to an authoritative problem solver so that collection is not disrupted.

- **Minimize the impact of data collection on library services**: Serve the user first.

- **Collect data unobtrusively where possible**: If library users pay more attention to data collection than their own activities, data collection results may change. The objective in all cases is to measure typical, representative activity.

- **Make it easy**: The easier it is to count the higher the likely quality. For example, if it is easy, staff may be more willing data collectors. None of the recommended measures require an advanced degree in statistics to collect or analyze.

- **Pretest**: Data collectors will make mistakes and have questions the first time; allow them the opportunity to learn from their efforts.

- **Keep your promises**: It may be difficult to motivate data collectors at some libraries because promises to explain what the measures mean, why they matter, what the results are, how the library compares with others, etc., were not kept in previous efforts. Keeping these promises is small compensation for the hard work involved.

The best data collection efforts find ways to encourage curiosity, keep it fun, balance the burden, and share the results.

Selecting "Typical" Weeks to Sample

Several of the recommended measures suggest that data collection be sampled for one week over a one-month period (Babbie, 1990). The data collected from the sample period is then used to make an annual estimate. For example, say there were 2,500 uses of the public access Internet workstations during the chosen one-week sample period. To obtain an annual figure multiply the 2,500 uses times 52 (weeks in a year). This equals an estimated 130,000 uses of the public access Internet workstations annually.

Sampling is a good idea because it reduces the burden on the data collectors and reduces counting error. However, the results are always estimates. Data coordinators need to choose sample periods that are normal, representative, and typical in order to improve the accuracy of the estimate. Using the above example, what week's activities are so typical that if you added them to obtain an annual total it would be closest to the actual annual total of uses of the public access Internet workstations? Common advice offered for choosing typical weeks includes:

- Pick a week that is neither unusually busy nor unusually slow,

- Choose a week in which the library is open regular hours,

- Avoid weeks with unusual events or holidays,

- Avoid periods with likely bad weather, and

- Consider seasonal differences in use.

Include seven consecutive calendar days from Sunday through Saturday (or whenever the library is usually open).

Obtaining Data from External Partners

Several of the recommended measures may require the library to obtain data from external partners including the ISP and licensed database and OPAC vendors. Typically these external partners collect the needed data using computer software. The use of external partners and computer software to collect data may be new to some librarians.

The ISP may be another unit of local government, or a local nonprofit organization, or a local business. An ISP routinely retains information that can be used to determine the number of virtual visitors to the library, for example, through the library's web page. The library's ISP will need to be contacted to obtain this data in order to use this recommended measure.

Vendors of licensed databases and library OPACs also retain data on the usage of databases. Libraries need this data to justify the expense of purchasing these services and to improve the quality of the services offered based on these databases. Discussions are already underway at state and national levels to encourage vendors of these databases to routinely provide needed data in a usable manner. Local libraries using such measures as: number of full-text titles available by subscription, number of database sessions, number of database queries/searches, and number of items examined using subscription services may have to contact their vendors in order to obtain the data needed for their library.

Log Analysis

One recommended measure, number of virtual visits to networked library resources, may make use of log analysis software to collect needed data on the Internet-based service usage. This software is still evolving in terms of added functionality. But already, log analysis holds great promise for better understanding of web usage.

The basics of log analysis software can be summarized briefly. Each time a user accesses certain Internet-based resources, for example, a web page, a brief record of the transaction is captured, ordered, and stored in a log in one or more files often called access log files on a computer (called a server) at the Internet service provider's. These log files can be loaded into a database and counted in various ways, for example, hits or virtual visits, and manipulated to produce other statistics. Appendix C provides sources for further reading and a partial list of producers of log analysis software.

Why Can't the Software Do It?

A frequent request from potential data collectors of the recommended measures is: why can't software be used to collect and analyze all of the data desired? Computer software is likely to be used to collect some of the recommended measures related to licensed databases and OPACs in the near future. This will reduce the burden on local data collectors. Further, the introduction and use of spreadsheet software to aid in local data analysis is becoming common. But in other areas related to electronic resources and services, software measurement is much less developed. The expectation that the software can do it all is unrealistic at present. A list of some of the software available to assist in data collection can be found in Appendix C.

DATA ANALYSIS AND USE

Chapter 2 of this manual recommends statistics that measure electronic resources and services and suggests potential uses for the results from each specific statistic by the local library, the State Library, and nationally. Chapter 3 suggests ways that these statistics can be further analyzed to provide additional descriptive insight. In some cases the recommended measures are combined or combined with existing traditional measures to form new composite measures. For example, the recommended statistic number of virtual visits excluding in-library use can be added to an existing count of physical attendance at the library to form a new composite measure: total library visits.

In other cases, a recommended measure is related using a ratio to another recommended measure or an existing traditional measure to produce a new performance measure. For example, the performance measure: public access Internet workstations per some amount of legal service area population. This performance measure is calculated by taking a traditional statistic, legal service area population, and dividing it by a new recommended statistic, number of public access Internet workstations in the library. This allows, for example, XYZ library to say it provides one public access Internet workstation per 3,000 persons in its legal service area.

Anticipate the Need to Explain the Results

The recommended measures of electronic resources and services, indeed the resources and services themselves, are new. Decision makers will need briefings before the release of the results from these recommended measures to help them understand what the results mean and what actions are suggested by the results. Planning for the release of the results from the recommended measures should begin as soon as the library selects from the list of recommended measures. Basic questions the library should ask include: What local purpose does the measure serve? Who needs to know the results from each measure? What are the consequences and actions to be taken if a measure's results make the library look good or if the results make the library look bad? How can I educate key library stakeholders about the measures chosen and the electronic resources and services they describe?

Estimates Are Better than Nothing, But They Are Still Estimates

One impetus for this manual was the widespread frustration with librarians' lack of knowledge about the impact of electronic resources and services on public libraries. As one successful library director remarked,

> With the advent of these new electronic resources and services in my library I am no longer confident that I really understand what is going on in my own building, let alone the branches. What are they [library users] using these resources for, why, and how can we help? I just don't know!

To begin the process of measuring electronic resources and services requires the willingness, over the near term, to estimate rather than try to obtain exact indicators. This approach is more than adequate for most library managers.

What this means for data analysis and use of the recommended measures can be summarized as follows:

- Librarians will have to become more sophisticated about what the results generated by the recommended measures do and do not suggest about the most appropriate course of action to take.
- Librarians will have to spend more time educating key decision makers about the meaning and limits of the results generated by the proposed measures.
- Librarians will have to tolerate the greater ambiguity of estimates as compared with the greater certainty of traditional library measures.
- Composite and performance measures that mix the traditional and new recommended measures are only as trustworthy as the least reliable data obtained.

Estimates with known limitations are better than no data at all. A great deal of attention is focused on improving the reliability, validity, and ease of collection of measures of electronic resources and services. But in the case of the present manual, estimates are better than nothing, but they are still estimates. Librarians need to know this and explain these factors to governing boards and other community members.

SOME FINAL THOUGHTS WHEN MANAGING DATA ANALYSIS AND USE

The sound advice developed and practiced by librarians over the years since the introduction of the first output measures manual remains useful when managing the measuring of electronic resources and services in today's public libraries. There are important differences in some of the management tasks required when collecting and analyzing the new, recommended measures and these are discussed above. These shifts in emphasis include:

- The need for careful selection of relevant measures from those recommended,
- Working with external partners to obtain necessary data,
- The use of computer software to collect and manipulate data for some measures,
- Additional instruction for data collectors and refocused attention on mechanisms for encouraging high quality data collection efforts, and
- Advance preparation and briefing of library administrators and key community stakeholders to better understand the implications of the new measures' estimated results for decision making.

But local library data coordinators who complete the federal, state, and Public Library Association annual surveys today should feel confident that they can handle the management of the recommended measures of electronic resources and services presented here.

6

Choosing Electronic Measures: Some Issues to Consider

The earlier chapters of this manual recommended new statistics and measures of electronic resources and services and ways to manage data collection and analysis. The present chapter addresses the increasingly likely situation that the measures here proposed are not sufficient for a library's needs. New information technologies, software applications, and patterns of use may demand new measures. International, national, and State Library and information organizations, as well as local library and information managers, will need to continue to develop and select new measures to respond to changing conditions. This chapter suggests issues for decision makers to consider when deciding whether to adopt a proposal for a new electronic measure. Figure 6-1 provides a work sheet for those deciding on a proposed new statistic or measure with key questions and a place for comments.

ISSUES TO CONSIDER

How Can You Reduce the Measure's Potential Error If You Can't Get Exact Data?

Developers of a new measure hope they will develop a measure that produces exact data and have that exact data matter. For example, some might want to state with a very high degree of confidence that the use of the Internet in public libraries in the United States increased by 23.457% over the previous year and that this increase

was the direct cause of increased funding of libraries by legislatures.

But is the production of such exact data an appropriate or even achievable goal in the near term? Few of the developers of electronic measures interviewed think such a goal is appropriate or achievable. The experts interviewed mention three principal areas of concern:

- The pace of new information technology and software application introduction into public libraries and the resulting change and impacts make the identification of useful measures, even with a utility of three to five years, difficult.

- Public libraries do not have the resources to commit, the staff with the necessary methodological knowledge base, or the staff with the necessary motivation, to sustain the methodological rigor necessary to achieve results at the highest confidence levels.

- The desire for data of the highest quality and upholding standards to obtain such data is stifling the production of necessary data, data of any reasonable quality at all, to inform the decisions on electronic resources and services that library managers need to make today.

Perhaps it is time to temporarily redirect the effort to produce exact data in the highly volatile environment of public library electronic resources and services in favor of the more pragmatic reduce-the-error approach when

FIGURE 6-1   Work Sheet for Choosing an Electronic Resources and Services Measure

Name of Proposed Measure:	
Questions to Ask	**Comments**
General Concerns	
How can you reduce the measure's potential error if you can't get exact data?	
What obstacles exist to the measure's implementation over its life cycle?	
Selection Issues	
What is the measure's purpose(s) and audience(s)?	
Can the definition be made clearer?	
Should you measure capacity, use, impact, or outcome?	
Is the measure essential, complete, and fair?	
Are you measuring something just because you can?	
What comparisons does the measure allow?	
How can the measure be used to enforce compliance, reward, or sanction?	
What is the potential for misuse?	
Data Collection Issues	
Are the data collection procedures clear?	
Can data for the proposed measure be collected from all relevant sources?	
Can you obtain needed data from your partners?	
Are new data collection techniques required?	
Is there a role for software in data collection?	
Are the library's confidentiality and privacy standards compromised?	
How can the burden of collection be balanced or reduced?	
Do the staff have the ability to collect the proposed measure?	
What preparation and instruction will be needed to collect the data?	
Data Analysis and Use Issues	
Can new and old be combined to produce composite and performance measures?	
Can nonlibrary produced data be integrated with the proposed measure?	
How should the results of a new measure be presented and to whom?	
What instruction will be needed to analyze and use the proposed measure?	
Does the cost of collection, analysis, and use exceed the benefit?	

considering a proposed measure of electronic resources and services.

Rather than develop and deploy the perfect measure the first time, the "reduce-the-error" approach seeks to produce new measures with a process in place for iteratively detecting, reporting, and correcting errors and limits so that the results may be better understood and trusted. The job of the researcher, whether at the state, national, or international level, or the local librarian collecting and using the resulting data shifts as well. As Katzer and his colleagues (1998, 8) suggest, "the researcher's job is first to identify, and then remove or reduce, sources of potential error so that findings can be trusted."

The spirit of the reduce-the-error approach is present in the introductory language of the 1999 ballot form introducing new network measures for the revised International Organization for Standardization international library statistics standard (ISO/CD 2789, iv):

> It is recognised that not all measures specified in this standard can be collected by libraries in particular sectors and of different size. The point of the specification is to ensure that where a particular statistic is collected the same definitions and methods are used.

The ISO study team identified a potential source of error: not all of the participating libraries could collect the data required for certain proposed measures at present. To reduce this potential source of error the ISO study team recommended two actions. First, ISO called attention to the problem. Second, even though not every library might be able to collect the data, ISO went ahead and proposed the standardized statistics anyway "to ensure that where a particular statistic is collected the same definitions and methods are used." With these efforts to reduce error, the new measures were deemed "good enough."

Librarians want accurate, credible, trustworthy, valid, and reliable data, but that does not mean that an estimate is not good enough. There was general recognition by study participants that at present there are a number of occasions when there are limited reliability and validity checks that can be established over the data collection process for new measures of electronic resources and services. Estimates, however, are better than having nothing. Estimates can still be used as input for decision making and are likely to be "good enough" as opposed to having no data. Clearly written reporting with precise definitions, good explanations, and identification of limitations reduces error and should be considered as an important component that can reduce the misinterpretation of such data in any data reporting process.

Questions for those using the reduce-the-error approach when selecting a new measure include: What are the potential sources of error for this new measure across its life cycle from selection through data collection, analysis, and use? Are there ways to reduce these potential sources of error through public disclosure of limits and reporting of problems during data collection and analysis? Is the proposed measure "good enough" given the known potential sources of error?

The list of issues to consider, summarized in Figure 6-1, offers a challenge. A developer of a new measure might well ask, why bother? No new measure can ever hope to successfully address all the issues raised in this chapter. Should this feeling occur, adopt the pragmatic, reduce-the-error approach. Any data, particularly data where the strengths and weaknesses are understood, are better than no data when a decision needs to be made. The issues presented here are designed to reduce error and increase utility, not stop new measure development.

What Obstacles Exist to the Measure's Implementation over Its Life Cycle?

Even experienced managers report that they made the mistake of selecting a measure because it was needed before assuring themselves that the library could surmount the potential barriers to local collection, analysis, and use. For example, the measure might look attractive as an aid to making an upcoming decision. But the systems unit is not familiar with the software required to collect data. Or, key staff will not be available during the sample period to collect the data. Or, negative results from the proposed measure may be easily misinterpreted.

Consider two useful strategies to avoid selecting a measure in isolation from the people and processes necessary to implement a successful measure. First, step through each phase of the measure's life cycle, from selection and data collection to data analysis and reporting and use. Are there barriers or obstacles at any point to successful local implementation? Second, involve the relevant staff in each stage of the process in the selection decision? For example,

- What do those who will collect the data think about the statistic, obstacles to data collection, the credibility of the results, etc.?

- Who will analyze the data? Do they think they have the resources needed to conduct the analysis?
- Who will use the results to make decisions? Do they understand the limits of the data?
- Who will be affected by the statistic's results? Do they trust the statistic to be fair?

The issues presented in the rest of this chapter are raised in their measurement life cycle order, from selection to data collection, data analysis, and use. A barrier to adoption may present itself at any point in a measure's life. Careful early planning can eliminate many obstacles. Considering the proposed measure's life cycle also increases library managers' abilities to assess the measure's worth when compared with the labor necessary to obtain and use the results.

SELECTION ISSUES

What Are the Measure's Purpose(s) and Audience(s)?

Be clear about a proposed measure of electronic resources or services purpose(s) and identify the specific audience(s) to whom the results will be communicated before selecting. How will the measure be used, for what purpose, to whom will the library present the measure's results?

Often measures are useful for many purposes with many audiences at different levels within the library and external to it. Some of these purposes include: better specifying what is occurring within the library, planning for library services, managing resource allocation, seeking library funding, gaining political advantage, shaping public opinion, educating the public, or developing policy, standards, sanctions, and rewards. A useful measure of electronic resources and services will positively contribute to achieving at least some of these purposes. Some of the audiences to be considered are: those who will collect the data, library managers, local boards and funding authorities, peer libraries, and local opinion leaders.

Do the statistic's results contribute to a solution to a local problem or might the results unnecessarily provoke, distract, or prolong the search for a solution?

- **Provoke**: Consider the case where the problem is well known and the statistic's results will not change the situation. A cautionary note: A rural librarian complained, "Why should I measure maximum bandwidth when everybody here knows that we won't be able to do better than a dial-up connection until our mom and pop phone company brings in fiber optic cable." While at the same time the State Librarian was remarking, "If I had that bandwidth data I could have convinced the legislature to subsidize fiber or other high bandwidth connections to those libraries who had been unable to obtain a fast connection." A careful assessment of the statistic and the situation it addresses may be necessary before accepting or rejecting a recommended measure.

- **Distract**: Consider the case where a library director has been told by the local governing authority that a major increase in a library's information technology budget is contingent on continued growth in the use of the Internet by library users. Should the library director switch from the locally accepted, but widely inaccurate, web site hits figure to number of virtual visits, which is more accurate but has a count lower than last year's hits figure? Will the new recommended statistic distract the governing board from authorizing the needed increase in funding?

- **Prolong**: One of the oldest techniques for delaying a decision or doing nothing is to demand more data. This technique can be especially successful if, after the data are obtained, they are found to be "unreliable."

Or, do you *intend* to provoke, distract, or prolong? Reconsider or drop the proposed measure of electronic resources and services if the measure's purpose does not connect with your purposes and that of key local stakeholders, be they those who collect the data, local funders, or your community's opinion leaders.

Can the Definition Be Made Clearer?

A proposed measure needs to be clearly defined for all its intended audiences. There are at least four related concerns:

- **Reliability**: The definition should be unambiguous to those collecting data so that it can be collected reliably. A reliable measure is one where everyone counts the same thing, the same way, every time. Local librarians, in particular, asked for clear definitions that included examples where possible.

- **Validity**: A valid measure fully measures what it intends to measure. There is the intent of the measure's constructors and the intent perceived by those who will use the measure's results to make decisions. Library managers need to assess the local agreement on this second type of intent early. Is there clear agreement among key local stakeholders about how the results (good or bad) will be used to make or support local decisions?

- **Communicability**: The measure's definition should be easily understood and communicated to its intended audiences. The study team delayed recommending several very useful, but highly technical, measures because they could not be easily communicated. The libraries' systems units easily understood the definitions but none of the other key decision makers did.

- **Usefulness for decision making**: A successful statistic yields unambiguous results leading to a preferred action. If a definition is unclear or subject to a range of interpretation, decision making becomes more difficult.

Pretest the measure's proposed definition with the audiences who will need to understand it. Is a lot of explanation of what the measure means or its significance necessary? Use of the measure may need to be dropped or delayed until an education effort is undertaken.

Should You Measure Capacity, Use, Impact, or Outcome?

When considering an area of library operations or services it may be useful to ask which would be most helpful, a measure of capacity, use, impact, or outcome? This question used to be phrased as, Should you use an input or output measure? A *capacity* measure is an input measure that describes the ability of a library to make use of an electronic resource or deliver an electronic service. Examples include the number of Internet workstations or the maximum speed of public access Internet workstations. A *use* measure is an output measure that describes the utilization of the library. Examples include the number of electronic reference transactions or visits to a library-created web site. An *impact* measure is a further extension of an output measure that describes the effects of library use. Examples include the number employed or the number of newly literate readers as a result of the library's electronic resources and services. Measures of

input, use, and impact do not necessarily depend on the library's explicit objectives and planning. An *outcome* measure is explicitly tied to the library's goals, objectives, and planning process. A good outcome measure provides data that tells a library manager if a specific library objective has been achieved.

Is the Measure Essential, Complete, and Fair?

This area of concern has three related parts:

- Does the measure extract what really matters, what you really want to know about the measure's subject? Can you do better?

- Does the measure (or a cluster of measures) comprehensively cover the measure's subject?

- Are other areas of the library's operations covered with equal or commensurate measurement attention?

Measuring can call attention, can suggest importance, and can enable easier or more confident administration. Not measuring ignores and neglects, suggests a lack of importance, and makes decision making in the area less precise and easy.

There are consequences to measuring some things and not measuring or being unable to measure others. For example, one senior administrator interviewed applauded the proposed new measures of electronic public services saying, "Finally we will begin to have equivalent quantitative evidence of what goes on in the public service area as we have had for some time in technical services." She went on to add that now maybe librarians can feel more confident that we are treating both sectors of the library equally.

What gets measured is limited because of the effort demanded of library staff, operations, and use. Getting to the essence of the phenomena and covering it fully is one challenge. Adequately and equitably measuring all library operational areas is another challenge.

Are You Measuring Something Just Because You Can?

The concern here is to avoid measuring something just because one can. Does the measure add value to the discussion? The danger of measuring because one can measure increases with the number and complexity of the criteria that must be passed in order to become a successful measure of electronic resources and services.

Keep in mind that each measure added increases the burden on library staff who must collect, analyze, and interpret the results. If the results are meaningless, all measuring activities are tarnished.

What Comparisons Does the Measure Allow?

A principal interest in statistics is for comparison. One common use is to compare library performance across time. Another popular use is to compare one library with other peer libraries.

Longitudinal data, looking at the results from the same measure over time, are useful to track trends within a library and as a check for unusual spikes or bad data. But the rapidly changing nature of information technology will have a substantial impact on the life cycle of measures of electronic resources and services. For example, it may not make sense to begin to track the number of modems a library owns today when it is likely that direct network connections will be the norm within the next five years. A good run of longitudinal data may now be three to five years given the rapidly changing information technology environment.

There is great interest in measures of electronic resources and services that can be used by libraries of different types because:

• Some data must be obtained from vendors who serve multitype libraries, not just the public library market. The measures' definitions and procedures must be useful to all library types, not just public libraries.

• Libraries, particularly in the licensed database area, increasingly participate in consortia and other networks. The measures' collection and use require interchangeability among all of the libraries participating, regardless of type.

• In some cases, adding data together from multitype libraries will be necessary. For example, a State Library might need this aggregated figure across all library types when seeking to renew state funding for licensed databases available to libraries within the state.

Co-development of measures of electronic resources and services with multitype libraries, networks, consortia, and vendors will be the norm if it is not already. New measures will need to be applicable to different types of libraries.

Peer comparisons with neighbors or with libraries that share some similar characteristics, within state or out-of-state, are one of the most popular uses of the existing annual survey statistics. For an example of a comparison of local libraries with out-of-state peers, see Loessner and Fanjoy (1996). But comparisons can be a blessing or a curse. Field-test participants told the study team of comparisons that led to divisiveness and ill will, of frustration when nothing was done or could be done to raise the standard of the lower tier libraries, and extensive wasted time when an unprepared media or public attempted to interpret the comparison. Peer comparisons are powerful tools but must be thoughtfully constructed and communicated.

Summarizing, these questions should be carefully considered: What comparisons do you want to make with the proposed measure? When considering a new measure of electronic resources and services, consider three to five years of potential longitudinal tracking a good run. Are your likely partners participating in the development of the measure? Do you have a plan for when the comparison is in your favor and when it is not?

How Can the Measure Be Used to Enforce Compliance, Reward, or Sanction?

Measures can be used to test compliance with various internal and external standards, regulations, and laws. Measure results can be used to determine resource allocation and funding. Careful early attention will be necessary to consider the likely outcomes of the use of any proposed measure of electronic resources and services to test compliance, reward, or sanction. For example, given a limited budget, how will you reward newly empowered staff with a new quantitative way of demonstrating their worth? Is the proposed measure another case of because we can measure it, we do?

What Is the Potential for Misuse?

Measures that must scale across governmental units, serve multiple purposes, and be useful across different types of libraries have an increased potential for misuse or misinterpretation. The intended purpose and intended audience for a measure may not be an unintended audience's purpose. A careful early assessment may avoid later pitfalls and improve the presentation and use of a proposed measure by advanced planning. Begin by identifying one way each proposed measure could be used to damage the library and who might use the measure in this fashion.

DATA COLLECTION ISSUES

Are the Data Collection Procedures Clear?

Comparisons across libraries require libraries to collect their data the same way; this in turn requires clear data collection procedures. Are the procedures in the proposed measure of electronic resources and services clear to those who will collect the data? If the procedures are not clear, then mutual agreement, discussion, and instruction may be needed before a potential measure can be adopted by all participating libraries.

Can Data for the Proposed Measure Be Collected from All Relevant Sources?

A library may face a wide array of potential sources of data when developing data collection strategies for a specific measure of electronic resources and services. For example, consider the collection of data on uses of public access Internet workstations just within one library. There might be different generations of equipment with different operating systems, with different application and data collection software, networks, and configurations. Developing a data collection strategy for a newly proposed measure might make the actual collection of data for a newly adopted measure possible.

Imagine the range of incompatible hardware, software, networks, configurations, not just in one library but across all participating libraries collecting data on a new measure of electronic resources and services. These incompatibilities and differences create a substantial challenge for the collection of the *same data* across all libraries using similar (but different) technology in various configurations. Producing exact data quickly devolves to reducing estimate error.

Avoid the "my technology, my outlook" syndrome: A library facility's local technology infrastructure and use of that technology leads to a local view of network statistics. That is, librarians base their need for electronic network statistics on their facility's use of and involvement with network resources and services. As such, it is often difficult for individual libraries to see the need for certain statistics and performance measures that do not *directly reflect* their facility's current implementation and use of various network services and resources.

Before adopting a proposed new measure of electronic resources and services, ask the relevant library staff:

- Do they understand the various issues involved?

- Can they identify all of the various sources of data related to the proposed measure?
- Can they develop strategies to collect the data from the range of sources involved? and
- What is their best estimate of time and cost to collect all the data?

Early discussions and lead time with relevant technical staff can reduce data collection problems later.

Can You Obtain Needed Data from Your Partners?

Partnerships, both formal (i.e., contractual) and informal, are a way of life for public libraries. But partnerships can create problems when trying to collect data for a new measure of electronic resources and services, particularly when the technology, network, or databases are not owned by the public library. Perhaps the most obvious case involves libraries and states that are engaged in substantial licensing agreements for Internet-based database access with vendors (e.g., OCLC, Ebsco, UMI, Gale/IAC). Another common example is when a library tries to obtain data collected by an Internet service provider (ISP) who may be another unit of local government or a private commercial firm.

Does the proposed measure require data owned by someone else or whose ownership needs to be negotiated? Are the data offered by a library partner a valid indicator of what it purports to measure? Are the offered data comparable with available data from other libraries? Can the data be obtained by using the definition and procedures required, when the data are needed, and at a reasonable cost? If the partner can not provide trustworthy data, on time and at an affordable cost, you may not be able to use the statistic.

Are New Data Collection Techniques Required?

A measure of electronic resources and services may require researchers and professionals to consider the benefits or necessity of using new data collection techniques including:

- Traditional quantitative methodologies (surveys or Likert scale surveys of user satisfaction with network services) in new ways.
- Less familiar qualitative (e.g., focus groups, interviews) methods.

FIGURE 6-2   Basic Criteria When Selecting an Appropriate Data Collection Technique

Criteria	Brief Discussion
Can the method provide appropriate data? may be more appropriate.	If you wanted to find out why users of the library web page spend their time in certain ways, interviews may be more appropriate than using log analysis software. If you want to find out how much time they're spending on various activities, activity log analysis software
Time needed for collection and analysis	For example, interview transcripts might take more time to analyze than log files.
Cost of collection and analysis	Costs may include costs of library staff, consultants to do data entry or analysis, and costs to users who may collect data for the researchers.
Instruction needed to collect and analyze	Both library staff and users may need to learn a new technique.
Degree of user involvement	The greater the involvement, the greater the likely time commitment or inconvenience required of users.
Commitment required of data collectors	The quality of the data collected may depend on the commitment of the data collectors.
Degree of representation of the data	For example, interviews with a few selected library users may not represent the range of views of the entire community.

- Traditional methodologies (e.g., pop-up web-based surveys).
- New methodologies (e.g., web-based transaction log analysis) to capture network usage data.

The use of multiple data collection techniques allows the library to cross-check the results and increase credibility and reliability.

In some cases, to promote timely and responsive measures it may make sense to rely on carefully developed samples rather than 100% population responses. In other cases, sequencing data collection, in which a question is not asked annually but every two or three years may be appropriate to reduce local data collection burden. Figure 6-2, based on McClure and Lopata (1996), offers some basic criteria when selecting an appropriate technique.

When considering a new measure of electronic resources and services, are new data collection techniques used and are they appropriate?

Is There a Role for Software in Data Collection?

The automation of aspects of the data collection and analysis processes holds great promise and threat for measurement of electronic resources and services. The promise is that one day measures of electronic resources and services will be collected and reported automatically and unobtrusively rather than through overt data collection efforts on the part of state and individual libraries. Already spreadsheet software is in common, productive use in the collection and analysis of library data. The threat is that libraries will wait until automatic data collection is perfected before collecting the data they need today to better manage electronic resources and services.

The "let the software do it" argument runs rampant among librarians considering new measures of electronic resources and services. However, software analysis and monitoring of network activities may be best characterized as in a pioneering phase. Librarians' awareness and familiarity with data collection and analysis software are minimal. There is limited capacity to develop (or apply) tailored software solutions within individual libraries and the profession as a whole. Indeed, finding available technical staff who can install and operate off-the-shelf solutions may be difficult. See Appendix C for examples of data collection and analysis software of potential use.

Are the Library's Confidentiality and Privacy Standards Compromised?

Many of the new electronic resources and services offered by the library simultaneously increase the opportunity for independent learning while reducing librarian awareness of what exactly the independent user does. This has several unintended consequences including:

- Librarians are less prepared to meet their users' needs because they are less certain what those needs are.
- Librarians are less certain of how to allocate resources among costly electronic resources and services because they are unsure how their users value them.
- Librarians are feeling greater compulsion to monitor patron use and their potential ability to do so is far greater with electronic resources and services.

Yet historically, many librarians have resisted collecting private or confidential data if for no other reason than that to do so would inhibit the independent learning that libraries seek to encourage.

Several questions regarding confidentiality may be worth addressing when considering a potential new measure. Would the methods used to collect data for the proposed measure violate library users' privacy or confidentiality? What do users deserve to know about the proposed measure's data collection and use? What choices should users have about participating in the process, about the use of the data, about the impact of resulting decisions? How unobtrusive should data gathering be? When does unobtrusive become secretive? Field-test librarians already report that many of their library users are very sensitive to being monitored when they use electronic resources and services. Does the proposed measure cause the library to reconsider historic written or unwritten agreements on user privacy and confidentiality? If so, are the results worth it?

How Can the Burden of Collection Be Balanced or Reduced?

The payoff for planning and decision making must be clear for those who collect the data in addition to those who use the data. Excessive burden on local library staff fosters "uncommitted record keepers." The result is, "The more statistics you ask me to collect, the more I'll make them up." Are the need and use of the proposed measure clear to those who will collect the data? Could

better procedures reduce the burden of data collection? Can incentives be found for data collection staff to ease the burden of collection? Collecting data that are, or appear to be, never used for decision making discourages collecting such data the next time.

Do the Staff Have the Ability to Collect the Proposed Measure?

Do the library staff that will be asked to collect data for the proposed measure have the ability to do so? Library managers and library system directors expressed concern that staff may not be able to:

- Engage in rigorous data collection activities that require staff time and effort;
- Support data collection activities with staff and resources;
- Develop expertise in electronic network data collection activities;
- Install and operate data collection and analysis software programs; and
- Collect any data other than that generated by system activity logs.

Essentially, the primary source of data collection—the library outlet level—may not have the ability, resources, or expertise to engage in electronic network data collection activities. Consider the abilities of the local public library staff to collect the data when examining a proposed measure. It is often the library that is least able to collect the data that stands to benefit most from the concrete evidence the data provide to decision makers and potential funders.

What Preparation and Instruction Will Be Needed to Collect the Data?

Collecting data about electronic resource and service measures will require lead time, preparation, and library staff instruction to be successful. There are a number of instruction topics that need attention, including:

- Identification of the range and diversity of technology that generates useful data relevant to a measure of electronic resources and services.
- Presentation of the notion that at least for the near term estimates, samples, and the lack of long-term longitudinal network data may be the norm.

- Introduction to new data collection techniques and how they may be applied to collecting network measures relevant to local libraries.
- Discussion of the impact of partnerships on collecting network data and presentation of strategies that can be used to overcome negative impacts. It may be wise to suggest to local libraries that they prepare their local partners for requests for network related data.
- Improvement of librarian knowledge of the strengths, weaknesses, and practical uses of existing software used to monitor network use. This may be done in concert with data entry instruction for the annual survey using the State Library's web site.
- Discussion of the utility of the network measures collected by library staff (who uses and how?). Where possible, connections need to be made between the network data collected locally and the resulting benefits to the local libraries.

Any set of new measures of electronic resources and services will require a "rollout" period that adequately educates and prepares libraries to collect the required data. Key activities that should take place during this rollout include instruction in the need for the data and how to collect the data properly, a dry run to pretest forms and procedures, discussion of what was learned with data collectors, and revision of forms and procedures.

What type of lead time preparation and what type of instruction will library staff need in order to effectively and efficiently collect data for the proposed new measure?

DATA ANALYSIS AND USE ISSUES

Can New and Old Be Combined to Produce Composite and Performance Measures?

Measure selectors must also consider whether a proposed measure can be compared to other measures both old and new. One promising way of analyzing data from new measures of electronic resources and services is to combine them with traditional measures to create *composite* measures of use. For example, number of virtual visits excluding in-library use can be combined with physical attendance at the library to form the composite measure: total library visits.

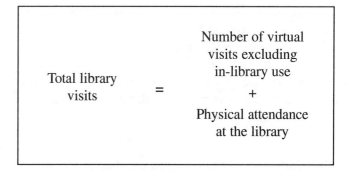

Another promising way of analyzing data from new measures of electronic resources and services is the use of performance measures. Performance measures relate one measure in proportion to another, oftentimes in a ratio. For example, the number of public access Internet workstation users is considered in proportion to the number of public access Internet workstations (by division) to form the performance measure: average annual use per workstation.

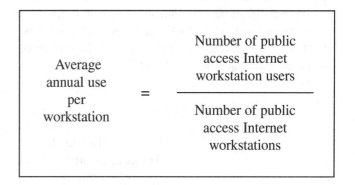

See Chapter 3 for further composite and performance measure examples.

The advantage of composite measures is that the resulting composite numbers represent more fully what libraries do. For example, the composite measure total library visits would show the increased library visits not indicated by the traditional physical attendance at the library statistic alone. The advantage of a performance measure is that it may clarify, reveal, or highlight previously ignored library activity. One of the field-test libraries used the average use per workstation data to determine where to place additional, newly purchased, workstations.

But there is a risk to be considered when using composite or performance measures. Perhaps the most important question to ask about composite and performance measures relates to credibility. Do you or key local stakeholders think you are combining or relating apples and oranges? If so, the credibility of the composite or performance measure is challenged and its utility may be reduced.

The key question is: Can the proposed measure be combined with others to form credible, useful composite or performance measures?

Can Nonlibrary-Produced Data Be Integrated with the Proposed Measure?

Libraries commonly combine results from traditional statistics (e.g., data from Federal State Cooperative System [FSCS] statistics) with data from government and private sources to enrich data analysis and enhance the presentation of a library's contribution to its relevant audiences. For example, a library might use its annual children's book circulation figure of 50,000 books and then obtain data from the U.S. Census Bureau. There are 10,000 children between five and seventeen years in the library's community using the Census Bureau's County Population Estimates by Selected Age Group. The results from both library and nonlibrary data could be used to obtain a children's circulation per capita figure of five books circulated per child.

$$\text{Children's circulation per capita} = \frac{\text{Number of children's books circulated (library-produced datum)}}{\text{Population between 5 and 17 (U.S. Census datum)}}$$

Additional examples using traditional statistics can be found in Appendix D, "Using Nonlibrary-Produced Statistics: A Bibliography."

One challenge facing public libraries today is to take the data produced from measures like the recommended ones in this manual as well as newly proposed measures and combine them in useful ways with data from other public and private sources. For example, the local newspaper reports that a private marketing firm has found that half the households in the community have Internet access. Current data from the U.S. Census indicates that there are 1,000 households in the community. Using results from the recently adopted measure number of virtual visits excluding in-library use of 80,000 visits, the library might make the following statement: the average household with Internet access in the community visited the library 160 times using the Internet last year.

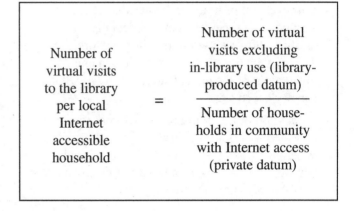

$$\text{Number of virtual visits to the library per local Internet accessible household} = \frac{\text{Number of virtual visits excluding in-library use (library-produced datum)}}{\text{Number of households in community with Internet access (private datum)}}$$

Can the proposed measure of electronic resources and services be integrated with nonlibrary-produced data to enhance their utility and persuasiveness?

How Should the Results of the New Measure Be Presented and to Whom?

A new measure of electronic resources and services should have an intended use and an intended audience, identified in advance. Potential audiences include:

- Library staff, particularly those who collected the data,
- Library governing boards,
- Other units of local government,
- Library funders,
- Users of libraries,
- Local media outlets,
- Peer libraries and state and national library organizations, particularly if the measure is locally developed.

Otherwise, why collect the data? What intended uses and audiences can you identify for the proposed measure? How should the results be presented for maximum effect?

What Instruction Will Be Necessary to Analyze and Use the Proposed Measure?

Librarians along with key library stakeholders will need help in analyzing and interpreting the results generated by a new measure of electronic resources and services. For example,

- Instruction may be necessary to analyze a new measure's results, particularly if new analysis software is used.
- Instruction may be necessary to interpret the results. Are the results good or bad? What do the results mean for the library?
- Instruction may also be necessary to develop new local ways to meaningfully and persuasively present the data.

Local governing boards and key opinion makers will need reeducation to increase the benefits from a new measure as well as to limit negative impacts. Librarians should expect to invest in instruction efforts with the introduction of any new measure. Who will require what type of instruction in order to better use the proposed new measure?

Does the Cost of Collection, Analysis, and Use Exceed the Benefit?

Library managers are well attuned to the cost of library activities. Figure 6-3 suggests one quick way of estimating costs and benefits for the proposed measure. There are likely to be other costs and benefits more relevant to the local situation. Start-up costs and benefits may be different than those that recur. But the work sheet in Figure 6-3 may well enable you to assess whether the cost of collection, analysis, and use exceeds the benefit.

ENHANCING THE SUCCESS OF MEASURES

This chapter raises issues that may need attention when selecting a potential measure of electronic resources and services. Choosing a useful measure requires a balance of thought and action. Some of the issues raised above will be particularly relevant to your situation and require thoughtful consideration. These concerns must be balanced by your need for some data, however imperfect and with known limits. Keep in mind the goal for any good measure is to improve decision making by reducing error, and then act. Select, use, and perfect measures that better the quality and usefulness of the library's electronic resources and services.

FIGURE 6-3   Estimating Costs and Benefits of Proposed Measure Work Sheet

Costs	Assign dollar amount (Comment if cannot)	Benefits	Assign dollar amount (Comment if cannot)
Administrative (to select, coordinate data collection, analysis, and use)		**Understanding** (clearer description and comparison lead to problem solving and new goals and objectives)	
Staff (time and salary to collect, analyze, and use data)		**Justification, Reward, Sanction** (results justify actions)	
Technology (e.g., costs to purchase, install, and use data collection and analysis software)		**Resource Allocation** (data enable better decisions)	

(continued)

Costs	Assign dollar amount (Comment if cannot)	Benefits	Assign dollar amount (Comment if cannot)
Instruction (Staff instruction in data collection, analysis, use. Stakeholder instruction in interpreting and using results)		**Quality** (data enable tangible improvement in services)	
Materials (for forms, reports, press releases, etc.)		**Savings** (data enable the library to save money)	
Intangibles (staff burden, negative publicity, disruption of services, postponed actions, etc.)		**Improved Image** (results improve image among key stakeholders)	
Other		**Other**	
Total		**Total**	

Extending the Use of Statistics and Measures for the Networked Environment

The rapid changes—and advances—in delivering information services and resources electronically pose critically important challenges to public libraries. These new techniques in the delivery of electronic and networked information have left many public libraries with inadequate data to make a range of decisions to provide cost-effective and high quality electronic services to their users. The lack of statistics and performance measures also severely limits the library's ability to adequately describe and represent its activities in the networked environment to governing boards.

The move to a networked environment has significantly increased the range of services and resources that the public library provides its users. The library has become a twenty-four-hour-a-day, seven-day-a-week access point to information services where users obtain services and resources on *their* terms and when *they* want such services—oftentimes *not* coming to the library physically nor interacting directly with library staff. The costs to provide these networked services and resources, however, can be significant.

On an experiential basis, most public librarians will describe the use of their networked information services with terms such as "exponential growth" or "we can't keep up with demand." At the same time, many public libraries have also seen stagnant or declining statistics of traditional indicators of library service such as turnstile counts, in-house reference transactions, and circulation.

This situation stresses the importance and need for the type of statistics and performance measures described in this manual. This manual offers a number of methods and statistics that have been carefully developed and tested to describe these services and resources. As such it will better help public librarians make good resource allocation decisions, meet user needs, and develop strategic plans for the development and operation of electronic resources and services.

A CHANGING CONTEXT

The evolving context in which public librarians will collect, analyze, and report statistics is considerably different than in the past:

- Librarians oftentimes do not control access and use to a range of data that describe vendor-supplied information services and resources. Some vendors are unwilling or unable to provide the types of statistics and use data that librarians request. Statistics and measures for database use and services, nonetheless, are essential.

- The rapidly changing technical nature of the networked environment also affects the types of services and resources that can be provided by libraries. As the networked services change, new types of statistics and measures may be needed.

- The level of effort needed to collect, analyze, and report data to produce statistics and performance measures for the networked environment may be greater than that needed to produce more traditional statistics.
- Software such as web server log analysis provides "automatic" counts and statistics of selected services and network activities (see Appendix C).
- Networked services, costs, and use may be difficult to "unbundle" if the library obtains these services through a consortium. Costs can either be hidden or be extremely difficult to allocate to individual libraries.

Librarians may be entering a period of time where statistics and measures for networked services may be useful for a limited time period and then will have to be redeveloped or discarded. Such an environment is quite different than the statistics-collecting environment in which public libraries previously existed. Despite these concerns and factors, public libraries can move forward and learn how best to produce and use such statistics and measures in this new environment.

A BEGINNING

The statistics and performance measures to describe public library services and resources in a networked environment described in this manual offer a beginning approach for public librarians to better meet user needs and provide better planning and decision making as to electronic and networked information services and resources. Public libraries must ensure that they are providing electronic resources and services that meet the needs of their various user groups—and if called upon to do so can justify the decisions made regarding these electronic services.

Using the techniques described in this manual, basic questions such as the following can be addressed:

- What specific statistics and performance measures might best describe use and users of electronic services in *my* library?
- What methods can be developed to determine who are the users, what are the uses of electronic information services and resources delivered by public libraries, and what is the frequency of that use?

- How can public libraries obtain timely, reliable, comparable, and useful data from database vendors that describe uses and users of the databases?
- To what extent can statistics and performance measures of electronic information services and resources be linked to a range of library outcomes?

The manual is best described as a guide—as opposed to a procedures manual—for how to use these statistics and measures. As suggested earlier, there are a number of issues that will still need to be considered in individual libraries when developing and implementing these statistics and performance measures.

ONGOING EVOLUTION OF STATISTICS AND PERFORMANCE MEASURES

Ultimately, networked statistics and performance measures for public libraries will continue to evolve because:

- The technology driving the delivery of networked services and resources will also continue to change radically—much of which we cannot predict;
- Some of the measures developed for today's environment may not be useful in tomorrow's networked environment, and new types of measures (e.g., number of compressed video-downloads) may be necessary; and
- National and state data collection reporting organizations such as the National Center for Educational Statistics (NCES) and State Library agencies may need new or different statistics to describe services and resources to policy makers.

Thus, public libraries should anticipate that the statistics and performance measures described in this manual will evolve, be refined and expanded, or perhaps dropped in the future.

This ongoing evolution of statistics and performance measures to describe services and resources in the networked environment will also require public librarians to become more knowledgeable about how the networked environment operates, the types of services and resources that can be provided, and how users interact with these services and resources. This increased knowledge will help librarians to extend the statistics and measures described in the manual for developing new statistics.

LINKING TO OTHER EFFORTS

Despite the limited number of writings and research available regarding the development of public library statistics and performance measures for the networked environment, significant progress is being made—and is likely to continue being made. Additional resources and background information can be obtained from <http://www.ii.fsu.edu> (the project home page).

In addition, the authors are working with the National Commission on Libraries and Information Science (NCLIS) on the project, Testing National Public Library Electronic Use and Network Performance Measures <http://www.nclis.gov/libraries/lsp/statist.html>. Building on the study described in this manual, additional work is envisioned to meet and collaborate with database vendors to determine the types of data that can be reasonably obtained for libraries. Public libraries' direct and formal involvement to participate in and extend these efforts to address public library database statistical needs and issues could build on existing work and demonstrate the interest and concern of the public library community.

Thus, an ongoing process of data collection, analysis, reporting, and decision making related to networked and electronic services is essential. The process described in this manual continues and extends the approach developed by the Public Library Association in earlier publications such as: *Output Measures for Public Libraries* (Van House et al., 1987), *Planning for Results: A Public Library Transformation Process* (Himmel and Wilson, 1998), *Managing for Results: Effective Resource Allocation for Public Libraries* (Nelson, Altman, and Mayo, 2000), and *Wired for the Future* (Mayo and Nelson, 1999). The use of statistics and performance measures described here can augment strategies and techniques developed in these related publications.

ONGOING EVALUATION FOR CONSTANT IMPROVEMENT

Statistics and performance measures to describe public library services and resources in the networked environment are tools. But an ongoing program of evaluation that regularly produces these statistics and performance measures is a tool essential for the long-term success of the library. These statistics and measures provide library decision makers with a means to:

- Describe the degree to which networked services and resources are accomplishing their stated goals and objectives;
- Assess the degree to which resource allocations for various networking services and resources are appropriate;
- Monitor the status and development of these services so that it is possible to make quick corrective actions;
- Identify the impact, benefits, importance, and problems with networked services and resources;
- Assist decision makers in determining whether to continue or modify existing services or develop new services;
- Provide objective information for justification of the services or otherwise demonstrate accountability for the program; and
- Educate decision makers, library staff, users, and others as to networked activities and services.

Perhaps most importantly, an ongoing program of evaluation contributes to the process of constant improvement—looking for ways to improve the usefulness, impact, and benefits that can result from networked information resources and services.

Indeed, constant improvement and development of library services is the hallmark of a successful public library. That such services are now, and will increasingly be, delivered via the networked environment is a sobering reality and significant change for public libraries. The selection of statistics and performance measures described in this manual can provide an important means for public libraries to continue delivering high quality services and resources via the networked environment.

MOVING FORWARD: DEVELOPING A NATIONAL PUBLIC LIBRARY ELECTRONIC RESOURCES AND SERVICES STATISTICS DATA COLLECTION MODEL

In developing this manual, a number of data collection issues surfaced that still require resolution. Among these issues are the:

- **Range of Sources of Electronic Resources and Services Data within an Individual Library:** No two libraries have the same information technology infrastructure, configuration, or systems implementation. This creates a substantial challenge for the collection of the same data from libraries using similar (but different) technology in various configurations.

- **Data Quality in an Era of Good Enough:** Librarians want accurate, credible, trustworthy, valid, and reliable data but that does not mean that an estimate is not good enough according to study participants. Indeed, all nationally collected and reported data related to libraries and services are best seen as estimates—even those that are currently collected (Library Research Service, 1995).

- **Limits to Longitudinal Data:** Longitudinal data are useful to track trends within a library and as a check for unusual spikes or bad data. But the rapidly changing nature of information technology will have a substantial impact on the life cycle of the electronic resources and services statistics and performance measures. It is very likely that it will not be possible to have longitudinal data that extend beyond three to five years—at most.

- **New Data Collection Techniques:** Electronic resources and services measures require researchers and professionals to consider the benefits and necessity of using new data collection techniques including traditional quantitative methodologies (surveys or Likert scale surveys of user satisfaction with network services) in new ways; less familiar qualitative (e.g., focus groups, interviews) methods; adapted traditional methodologies (e.g., pop-up web-based surveys); and newly created methodologies (e.g., web-based transaction log analysis) to capture network usage data. In some cases, to promote timely and responsive measures it may make sense to rely on carefully developed samples at the local, state, and national levels rather than 100% population responses. In other cases, sequencing data collection, in which a question is not asked annually but every two or three years may be appropriate to reduce local data collection burden.

- **Burden of Collection:** It is not clear if there are adequate rewards and incentives for state library and individual libraries to initiate a regime of collecting new networked statistics and performance measures given other demands on their time. It is necessary to reexamine the assumption that local libraries will continue to participate in the annual surveys that include additional data collecting requirements related to networked services and resources without such incentives.

- **Ability of Local Libraries to Collect Electronic Resources and Services Measures:** In order to attain national electronic resources and services statistics and performance measure data, it is necessary to collect the raw data at the local library outlet level. An issue raised in the study's data collection activities is the ability of the library outlets to collect such data. Indeed, branch library managers and library system directors expressed concern regarding the ability of their facilities to do so.

- **Preparation and Training Necessary:** Collecting data about electronic resources and services measures will require preparation and library staff training to be successful. There are a number of training topics that need attention including the identification of the range and diversity of technology generating network measures; the notion that at least for the near term estimates, samples, and the lack of long-term longitudinal network data may be the norm; and introduction to new data collection techniques and how they may be applied to collecting network measures relevant to local libraries.

- **Training in New Data Analysis Techniques Necessary:** Training in how to analyze and interpret these new electronic resources and services measures (some more than others) will be necessary at all levels. For example, training librarians to download preformatted data into a standard spreadsheet and then do some basic analysis. In addition, few of those interviewed outside of some systems librarians knew how to use network analysis data effectively. In the case where the library has systems staff, electronic resources and services data may only be used for internal technical purposes. Often, however, these technical experts have not seen the utility of these data for wider administrative purposes such as demonstrating use, showing need, garnering funding.

- **Training in the Analysis and Use of the Electronic Resources and Services Data Reported Necessary:** Librarians have spent decades convincing local governing boards that circulation counts, attendance records, reference transactions, etc., that go up annually are a "good thing." Now that these and other traditional counts are stagnant or declining in many cases, librarians have to reeducate governing boards that web hits, electronic reference questions, full-text downloads, and other indicators are as or more important than the traditional measures.

- **Partnerships—Maintaining Control, Obtaining Data:** Partnerships, both formal and informal, are a way of life for public libraries. But they can create problems for the collection of needed electronic resources and services measures when the technology, network, or databases are not owned by the library (i.e., owned by online database vendors).

These issues, at a minimum, require attention and an acceptable level of resolution for it to be possible to develop and collect national public library network statistics and performance measures.

POSSIBLE MODELS FOR NATIONAL DATA COLLECTION

The ability to resolve several of the issues identified above lies, in part, with the type and nature of the national public library electronic resources and services statistics and performance measure system adopted by library professionals, researchers, and policy makers. There may be numerous approaches to the development of a national network statistics and performance measure collection, reporting, and analysis system. These include:

- **Extending the current National Center for Education Statistics (NCES), National Commission on Libraries and Information Science (NCLIS)**, State Library agency, and public library Federal State Cooperative System (FSCS) collaborative approach for annual public library data collection. In this model, public library data on selected statistics are passed from public libraries to State Library agencies up to NCES for compilation, analysis, and reporting. All fifty states plus the District of Columbia and U.S. territories participate in the process.
- **Developing a lead states-and-libraries approach to data collection and reporting**. For a variety of reasons, it may not be feasible for all public libraries and State Library agencies in the nation to simultaneously adopt and report data on a set of electronic resources and services statistics and performance measures. However, throughout this manual development process, a number of states indicated their willingness or desire to collect at

least a core set of electronic resources and services statistics and performance measures from the public libraries within their states. Also, while a State Library agency or a number of public libraries within a state may not be willing or able to collect electronic resources and services statistics, lead public libraries within states may find it imperative to collect such data for a variety of decision-making, management, and reporting purposes. In this model, lead public libraries and State Library agencies adopt, collect data, analyze data, and report data on a core set of network statistics and performance measures. The lead State Library agencies and public libraries also serve as an incubator for developing, defining, and reporting new network statistics and performance measures.

- **Creating an ongoing sampling design to generate national estimates**. This model employs a sampling approach for a variety of data collection activities to use with public libraries, State Library agencies, and library network consortia. The intent of this approach is to develop a sample that would enable the generation of national estimates of a core set of electronic resources and services statistics and performance measures from public library, State Library agency, and library network consortia. Such a model would permit the targeting of network statistics appropriate to the level of data collection—library, State Library agency, library consortia—as well as a framework for modifying or creating new statistics and performance measures on an as-needed basis. It would be possible to engage in the data collection process on a regular (e.g., annual, biannual) or ad hoc (i.e., as necessary) basis.
- **Adopting a combination approach to network statistic and performance measure data collection.** The above data collection models are not mutually exclusive. Rather, it is possible to combine aspects of the FSCS, lead state/library, and sampling approaches to collect, analyze, and report public library electronic resources and services statistics and performance measures so as to provide nationally aggregated network statistical data.

Other models may exist, but the above serve as illustrations of possible ways to begin collecting, analyzing, and reporting electronic resources and services statistics and performance measures nationally.

While it is not possible at this time to determine which approach(es) is (are) most appropriate for collecting national electronic resources and services statistics and performance measures, some key characteristics should include:

- **Creating a fast response approach to the development, collection, analysis, and reporting** of electronic resources and services statistics and performance measures. A key criticism of the FSCS process is the time lag between the development of data elements and the eventual reporting of those elements. For a variety of reasons, it can take three years under the current FSCS process from development to reporting of statistics (to be fair, the FSCS group undertook changes in its bylaws recently to expedite the element adoption and reporting process). By the time the NCES releases the public library data reports, the data are often outdated. This is particularly problematic in the networked environment in which any network statistics and performance measures will likely remain relevant for a limited time period.

- **Fostering an environment of constant change**. Gone are the days of statistics and performance measures that last for decades. The networked environment is such that change in technologies and the implementation of those technologies are rapid. Thus, the statistics and performance measures that capture electronic resources and services data will necessarily undergo constant modification. It is imperative, therefore, that the model for national library network statistics and measures foster an environment of flexibility, change, and creativity in the creation, collection, and reporting of statistical data.

- **Implementing a reasonably burden-free data collection and reporting process for public libraries**, State Library agencies, and library consortia. It is clear that data reporting requirements imposed on public libraries are arduous. It is also clear, however, that electronic resources and services usage statistics are increasingly important to professionals, researchers, and policy makers. Thus, it is necessary to develop a data collection and reporting system that provides maximum benefit for minimal effort.

- **Working with nonlibrary partners to gain access to library electronic resources and services data.** Increasingly, key network usage data are out of the public library, State Library, and library consortia domain. Examples include online database usage, Internet service provider (ISP), and telecommunications carrier (e.g., bandwidth consumption) data. It is critical to the measurement of library network services that the national data collection activities develop reporting partnerships with, minimally, the online database vendor, ISP, and telecommunications carrier communities.

There are likely other characteristics necessary for a national public library electronic resources and services statistics and performance measure data collection system, but the above are key.

This manual's primary focus is to provide the public library community with an initial road map to the collection, analysis, reporting, and usage of electronic resources and services statistics and performance measures. Readers will hopefully incorporate the suggestions presented in this manual into their library's existing data collection activities—or begin developing a systematic and meaningful data collection system. A well-executed data collection system, as part of a larger planning and evaluation effort, can provide libraries with valuable data regarding library electronic resources and services usage. Such data are essential for public libraries to be successful in the future.

APPENDIX A

Statistics and Measures Needing Further Consideration

The following includes statistics, composite measures, and performance measures needing further consideration before the study team can recommend them for general use. Individual libraries may wish to consider these measures for their own use or in conjunction with system or peer library use. *Note:* All items presented here have proposed definitions. In addition, some items have procedures and other details supplied.

Percentage of Legal Service Area Population Accessing the Internet via the Public Library

Definition: Divide the number of virtual visits by legal service area population and then multiply by 100.

$$\text{Percentage of legal service area population accessing the Internet via the public library} = \frac{\text{Number of virtual visits}}{\text{Legal service area population}} \times 100$$

Number of Virtual Materials Used (Include Itemized Virtual Materials Use Report)

Definition: Annual count of the book-circulation equivalent use of electronic materials including:

- Full displays of a citation with abstract (exclude citation only display),
- E-mails sent or read using public access Internet workstations,
- Count of chat room use by participant,
- Display of full text of a document,
- Intensive web page accesses lasting more than X minutes or with penetration greater than one level,
- Displays of graphics from a graphic database like AP Photo Archives,
- Count of audio files played,
- Electronic documents delivered (if not counted in interlibrary loan items borrowed),
- Downloads or prints of any item from any electronic source including CD-ROM or Internet sources (including licensed databases and web accessible resources),
- Other or new book circulation equivalents not mentioned here.

Some of the above items may be sampled rather than counted continuously. Every local library may not be

FIGURE A-1   Itemized Virtual Materials Use Report to Accompany Number of Virtual Materials Used

Book-Circulation Equivalent Electronic Use	Count or Comment (indicate if could not count, count as zero if service not provided)
Full displays of citation with abstract	
E-mails sent or read	
Count of chat room use by participant	
Display of full text of a document	
Intensive web page accesses	
Displays of graphics	
Count of audio files played	
Electronic documents delivered	
Downloads or prints	
Other equivalents (indicate what was counted)	
Total	

able to count every book-circulation equivalent use so it will be necessary to attach the itemized virtual materials use report to this statistic for comparison purposes (see Figure A-1).

Procedures: Local libraries also may not be able to count all electronic book-circulation equivalent uses at present because:

- A noninvasive means may not exist,
- The local library may not have the software or skill to use it,
- Library partners such as licensed database vendors may be unable or unwilling to supply needed data, etc.

But they should report what they can, knowing that each item reported improves the accuracy of the measure and the total materials used count. What follows are sug-

gested collection procedures for each of the items identified in the Itemized Virtual Materials Use Report, above.

Number of Electronic Books to Which the Library Subscribes or Owns

Definition: Count of the number of electronic books which the library owns or has through subscription computed annually. Excluded from this statistic are electronic texts freely obtainable via the Internet.

Procedure: Request from e-book subscription vendor(s) a current machine-readable list of full-text titles offered to which the library subscribes. Combine the machine-readable lists and add a list of the e-books owned by the library. Eliminate any duplicates and obtain a total count of unique e-book titles.

Number of Virtual Visits after Hours

Definition: Using the same virtual visit definition recommended in Chapter 2, track visits when the library buildings are closed and not providing traditional services.

Number of Virtual Library Visits Compared with Other Web Services

Definition: Using the same virtual visit definition recommended here, compare the library virtual visit statistic with similar figures from other web pages. For example, compare the virtual visits from the library web page to those from the local city government web page or school district web page or other community service web pages.

Location of Virtual Visit to Library

Definition: In order to know how far electronic library services enlarge the range of library services and increase their market penetration, it is important to know the provenance of each use. Three "locations" should be differentiated:

1. inside the library;
2. outside the library, but inside the institution or authority (population to be served);
3. outside the institution or authority (population to be served).

Proposed ISO measure (2000, A.2.2).

Reasons for inaccuracy: Uses inside the library may include those by external users (outside the population to be served), so that locations 1 and 2 together would not always show the exact number of uses by the population to be served. It may be difficult to distinguish between remote uses by the population to be served and remote uses by external users. Reliable results can be obtained from access systems requesting identification for every login. Controlled access is always needed for bought or licensed services, and identification/authentication systems will probably be introduced widely to resolve this problem.

Average Web Page Loading Response Time

Definition: An estimated average response time of public access workstations when loading a standardized test graphically intensive web page.

Procedure: At opening and at 4 PM for one week, the library will load a web page found at [designated site, say, PLA]. Using a stopwatch, count the time it takes from loading the URL until page is fully loaded for each measurement. Add all measurements and divide by the number of measurements to obtain the average web page access response time.

Percentage of Public Access Workstations in Use

Definition: A sampled average of the number of public access Internet workstations in use during one week.

Procedure: Each day for one week take three measurements at representative times. At each measurement, observe the number of public access Internet workstations in use. Average the workstations in use each day and for the week.

Licensed Database Subscription Expenditures

Definition: Total expenditures for licensed database(s) subscription. May include one-time start-up costs as well as recurring costs.

Collected by: Library supplies.

Survey Period: Measure once annually.

Procedure: 1) Calculate the one-time start-up fee(s) for each licensed database. An example is the total cost of a site license for a database; and

2) Calculate the recurring cost(s) or fee(s) for each licensed database. An example is the total annual subscription cost for a licensed database.

3) Consider using the work sheet shown in Figure A-2.

Search Time

Definition: Search time is defined as the period between a login to and a logoff (intentional or unintentional) from an electronic service. This count gives additional information on the intensity of use of a certain service. Proposed ISO measure (2000, A.2.1.4).

Reasons for inaccuracy: The search time depends on many variables. These include the ease of handling (manuals, online help functions, and self-explanatory menus) and users' experience. A long search time, therefore, does not always reflect users' interest in the service.

FIGURE A-2 Work Sheet for Licensed Database Subscription Expenditures

One-Time Fee(s)	Itemize Each Fee
$	
$	
$	
Total one-time fee(s)	
Recurring Fee(s)/Cost(s)	**Itemize Each Fee**
$	
$	
$	
Total recurring cost(s)/fee(s)	

Rejected Logins

Definition: A rejected login is defined as an unsuccessful login to an electronic service where it is unavailable for operational reasons, e.g., requests exceeding simultaneous user limit. Failure of login because of technical reasons (e.g., system breakdown) or wrong passwords is excluded. This dataset shows how far the simultaneous user limit is sufficient for users' interests. Proposed ISO measure (2000, A.2.1.5).

Reasons for inaccuracy: The number of logins exceeding the simultaneous user limit cannot always be differentiated from other rejections, e.g., missing or mistyped passwords.

Average Number of Repeat Visits per Month

Definition: Average of the counts of repeat visits to the library's web page during a month's period.

Special Consideration: Requires a large amount of memory because of the log analysis database created.

Analysis and Use: Are virtual visitors to the library one-time users? Does the library web page continue to be relevant?

Number of New Visitors to Public Library Using Public Access Workstations

Definition: Count of the number of new (not previously registered) visitors to the public library who use its public access workstations.

Procedure: Use a sample, for example, two weeks over a selected two-month period, to produce an annual estimate. Use a sign-in log sheet for access to public access workstations during the sample period. Compare sign-ins with registered borrowers and count those sign-ins who are not registered borrowers.

Access to Information Technology

Definition: Count of access to selected information technologies at public library outlets indicating whether access is free or for fee.

Procedure: Put an X next to each information technology that the library makes available to the public whether for free or for a fee (see Figure A-3). For a library system, answer this question for the individual library (main and branches; do not count bookmobiles) and compute a system average by adding the totals from each outlet and dividing by the number of outlets.

FIGURE A-3 Report Form for Access to Information Technology Data Element

Place an X in the categories that apply at your library and total at the bottom.

Information Technology Offered to the Public	Offered to the Public	Offered at the Library for Free	Offered at the Library for a Fee
Telephone			
Copy machine			
Tape cassette machines for loan			
Facsimile machine			
Television			
CD-ROM reader			
CD-ROM writer			
CD-ROM player (for music, etc.)			
DVD player			
VCRs			
Scanner (not scantron)			
Adaptive or assistive device			
Loan of camcorder			
Loan of digital camera			
Standalone personal computers			
Public access Internet workstations			
Computers attached to a local area network			
Library web site			
Library maintained computer lab suitable for group training or distance learning			
E-books and readers			
Totals			

Access to Information Technology-Based Services

Definition: Count of access to selected information technology-based services at public library outlets for free or for a fee.

Procedure: Put an X next to each information technology that the library makes available to the public whether for free or for a fee (see Figure A-4). For a library system, answer this question for the individual library (main and branches; do not count bookmobiles) and compute a system average by adding the totals from each outlet and dividing by the number of outlets.

Number of Reference Questions Answered Using the Internet

Definition: Count of the use of the Internet by public library reference staff to answer reference questions in full or in part. For example, use of a web page or licensed database available on the Internet and e-mailed question or answer.

Procedure: Use a sample, for example, one week over a selected one-month period, to produce an annual estimate. This question can be added to the standard reference tally sheet. Count each use of the Internet by public library reference staff to answer reference questions in full or in part. Be sure to include virtual reference transactions received and answered remotely.

Percentage of Reference Questions Answered by Reference Staff Using the Internet

Definition: Divide number of reference questions answered using the Internet by total reference use and then multiply by 100.

Number of Independent User Activities

Definition: Count of the number of independent user activities formerly requiring library assistance. Examples include: self-circulation checkout, telephone or web renewals, placing of holds on library materials, user-placed interlibrary loans, downloads of forms, number of virtual visits to networked library resources and number of database queries and searches.

Collected by: Library collects.

Survey Period: Local library chooses two weeks within a selected two-month period once a year. One week equals the number of hours the library is open during a consecutive seven-day period and may vary across libraries surveyed.

Procedure: 1) Identify all of the independent user activities formerly requiring library assistance and determine which activities are already counted in some way.

2) Arrange to count those activities not currently counted during the sample period as appropriate.

3) Combine the totals of these various independent user activities into a total count.

Analysis and Use: Many libraries seek to promote themselves as available even when the library building is closed. This statistic is an indicator of library activities that take place independent of library staff. Libraries also seek to promote the notion that, with the advent of new information technologies, using the library is more convenient. This statistic highlights new and convenient services and how many people are using them.

Number of Staff Hours Preparing for Information Technology User Instruction

Definition: Count of the number of hours that reference staff spend preparing for information technology user instruction. Preparation examples include: developing curricula, creating instructional materials, organizing presentations, etc. Specifically excluded are the hours spent actually instructing users. See instead user information technology instruction: number of hours of information technology user instruction recommended in Chapter 2.

Average Staff Preparation Time Devoted to Information Technology User Instruction

Definition: The average staff time spent preparing for one contact hour of information technology user instruction.

$$\text{Average staff preparation time devoted to information technology user instruction} = \frac{\text{Number of staff hours preparing for IT user instruction}}{\text{Number of hours of information technology user instruction}}$$

FIGURE A-4 Report Form for Access to Information Technology-Based Data Element

Place an X in the categories that apply at your library and total at the bottom.

Information Technology Services Offered to the Public	Offered to the Public	Offered at the Library for Free	Offered at the Library for a Fee
Word processing software available			
Database software available			
Spreadsheet software available			
Presentation software available (including graphing, clip art graphics) (e.g., Powerpoint)			
Desktop publishing			
Web page creation software			
Online retrieval of database information (via CD-ROM or Internet)			
E-mail reading/writing permitted			
Chat sessions permitted			
Web pages from community members housed on library equipment			
Availability of library-sponsored listserv™			
Learning modules (including educational games, integrated learning systems, drill, practice, tutorials, simulation) available			
Formal information technology training sessions offered regularly			
Group training using computer lab available			
Telephone messaging center			
Video production capability			
Library as an Internet service provider (ISP)			
Totals			

Number of Users of Electronic Resources and Services

Definition: This composite figure combines several new electronic statistics including: number of virtual visits to networked library resources, number of users instructed in information technology and number of virtual reference transactions to begin to estimate the number of users of public library electronic resources and services.

Calculation: Add number of virtual visits to networked library resources, number of users instructed in information technology and the number of virtual reference transactions together.

$$\text{Total amount network services provided} = \text{Number of virtual visits to networked library resources} + \text{Number of users instructed in information technology} + \text{Number of virtual reference transactions}$$

Analysis and Use: This composite measure provides an estimate of the number of users in this important new area of public library service.

Analyzing Vendor Statistics

This appendix walks users through importing vendor-provided online database usage statistics into Microsoft Excel for analysis purposes. In particular, it demonstrates how to import the number of electronic network items examined for Ebsco and UMI/Bell & Howell, based on the field test conducted for this statistic during the development of the manual. The tutorial instructs users on how to:

- Obtain the usage report;
- View the usage report; and
- Analyze data in the usage report.

Each category is discussed below. Please keep in mind that the procedures and usage reports provided by the vendors change continuously and will continue to do so. This appendix describes analysis procedures as of June 2000.

OBTAINING THE USAGE REPORT

Ebsco

Subscribers to Ebsco's licensed databases can obtain usage reports from Ebsco's administration web site. The subscriber needs a customer ID and password to view one of four reports: session, database, title, and IP.

Figure B-1 displays the database usage report screen from the Ebsco web site. Ebsco allows its subscribers in most reports to select a:

- Consortium site;
- Detail level;
- Database;
- Time period; and
- Fields to show.

After one of the above is selected, subscribers can either view the report online or e-mail it to themselves. Figure B-2 displays the e-mail report screen. Subscribers must enter their e-mail address and select an output format that is either HTML, comma-delimited, or tab-delimited. Select any of the output formats to download data into an Excel spreadsheet for statistical analysis.

An important feature on the Ebsco e-mail report screen is the frequency option. Subscribers can either obtain a usage report by visiting the Ebsco web site monthly or have the usage reports automatically e-mailed to them on a preselected month and day.

UMI/Bell & Howell

UMI/Bell & Howell sends its usage reports via e-mail monthly to its database subscribers.

FIGURE B-1   Ebsco's Database Usage Report Parameters Screen

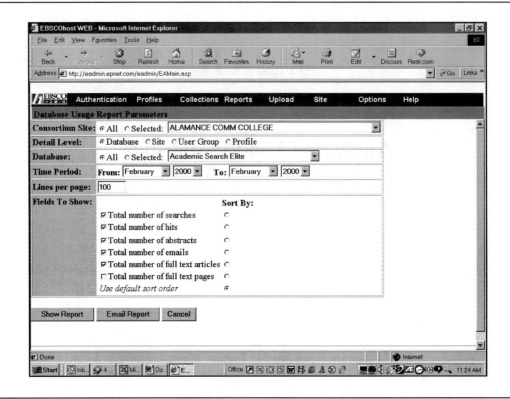

FIGURE B-2   Ebsco's E-mail Database Usage Report Screen

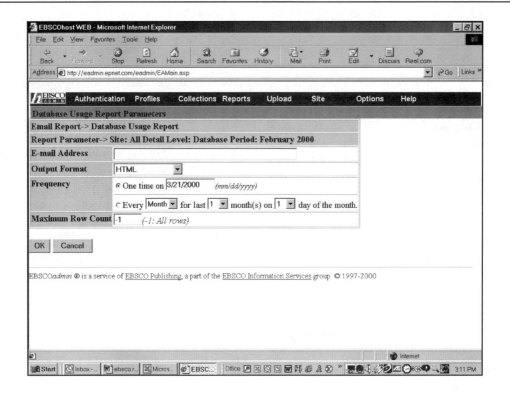

FIGURE B-3 Ebsco's Database Usage Report in Excel

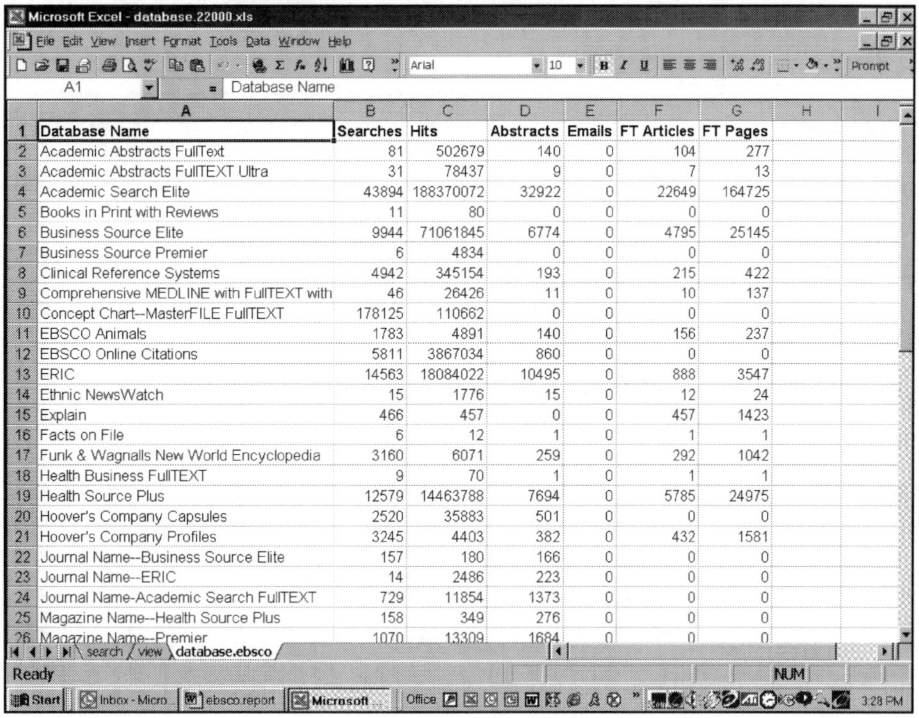

Database Name	Searches	Hits	Abstracts	Emails	FT Articles	FT Pages
Academic Abstracts FullText	81	502679	140	0	104	277
Academic Abstracts FullTEXT Ultra	31	78437	9	0	7	13
Academic Search Elite	43894	188370072	32922	0	22649	164725
Books in Print with Reviews	11	80	0	0	0	0
Business Source Elite	9944	71061845	6774	0	4795	25145
Business Source Premier	6	4834	0	0	0	0
Clinical Reference Systems	4942	345154	193	0	215	422
Comprehensive MEDLINE with FullTEXT with	46	26426	11	0	10	137
Concept Chart--MasterFILE FullTEXT	178125	110662	0	0	0	0
EBSCO Animals	1783	4891	140	0	156	237
EBSCO Online Citations	5811	3867034	860	0	0	0
ERIC	14563	18084022	10495	0	888	3547
Ethnic NewsWatch	15	1776	15	0	12	24
Explain	466	457	0	0	457	1423
Facts on File	6	12	1	0	1	1
Funk & Wagnalls New World Encyclopedia	3160	6071	259	0	292	1042
Health Business FullTEXT	9	70	1	0	1	1
Health Source Plus	12579	14463788	7694	0	5785	24975
Hoover's Company Capsules	2520	35883	501	0	0	0
Hoover's Company Profiles	3245	4403	382	0	432	1581
Journal Name--Business Source Elite	157	180	166	0	0	0
Journal Name--ERIC	14	2486	223	0	0	0
Journal Name-Academic Search FullTEXT	729	11854	1373	0	0	0
Magazine Name--Health Source Plus	158	349	276	0	0	0
Magazine Name--Premier	1070	13309	1684	0	0	0

VIEWING THE USAGE REPORT

Once the usage reports are sent and received by the subscribers, the information is downloaded into a spreadsheet program such as Microsoft Excel. The format of the report, delimited or HTML, determines how it is downloaded into Excel. A step-by-step procedure of how to view Ebsco's and UMI/Bell & Howell's usage reports is discussed below.

Ebsco

As previously mentioned, subscribers can choose which format to receive their e-mail report in. If a subscriber selects the HTML format, the usage report normally is opened in Excel. Usage reports are also available in a tab- or comma-delimited format. To view a tab- or comma-delimited report, follow the directions in Excel's Text Import Wizard Screen. Figure B-3 is an example of Ebsco's database usage report in Excel after import.

UMI/Bell & Howell

Subscribers that receive usage reports from UMI/Bell & Howell receive a tilde (~) delimited report to import into Excel. To view a tilde (~) delimited report, follow the directions in Excel's Text Import Wizard Screen. Figure B-4 shows the usage report in Excel after import.

ANALYZING THE USAGE REPORT

The data as received from both Ebsco and UMI/Bell & Howell do not display information on the number of electronic network items examined in a user-friendly format. However, with manipulation of the data in the usage reports it is possible to obtain the number of views by host and by database. Go into Excel's PivotChart Wizard to create the sum of each view per database and sum of total views per database. Figures B-5 and B-6 display the results for the number of electronic network items examined, manipulated in Excel for Ebsco and UMI/Bell & Howell.

FIGURE B-4 UMI/Bell & Howell Usage Report

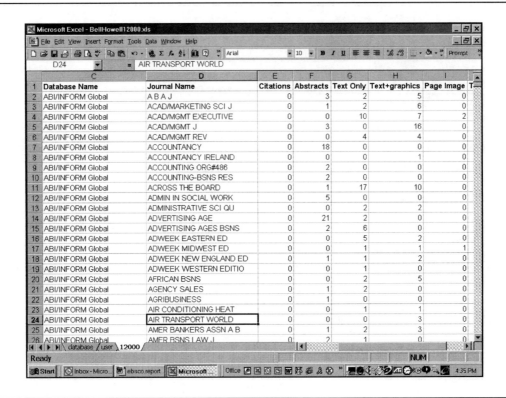

FIGURE B-5 Number of Views per Database: Ebsco

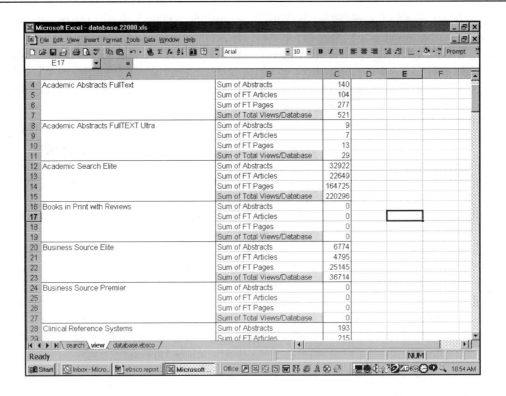

FIGURE B-6 Number of Views per Database: UMI/Bell & Howell

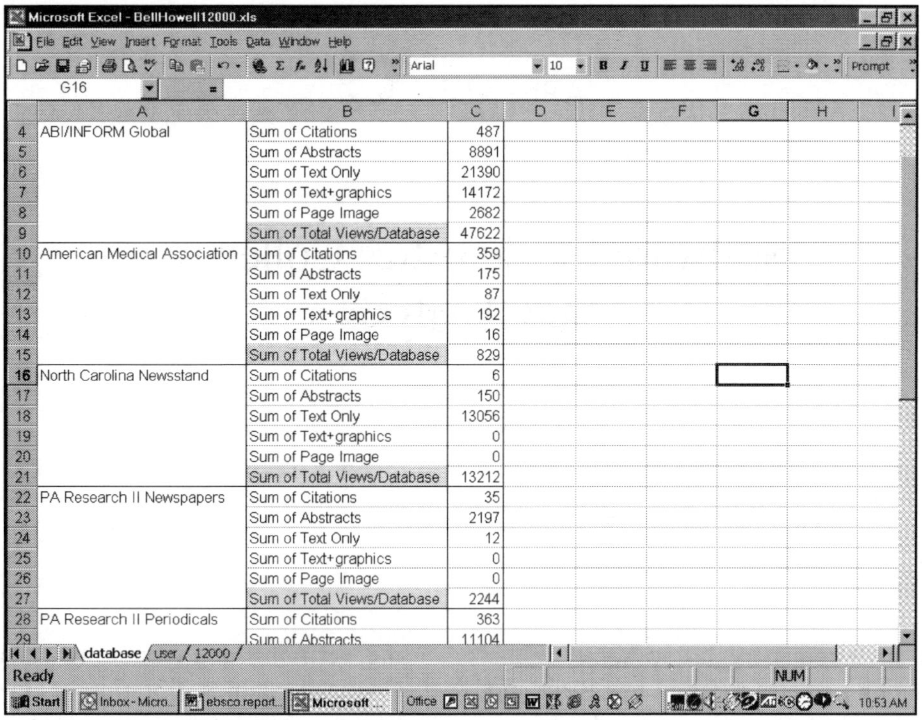

	A	B	C
4	ABI/INFORM Global	Sum of Citations	487
5		Sum of Abstracts	8891
6		Sum of Text Only	21390
7		Sum of Text+graphics	14172
8		Sum of Page Image	2682
9		Sum of Total Views/Database	47622
10	American Medical Association	Sum of Citations	359
11		Sum of Abstracts	175
12		Sum of Text Only	87
13		Sum of Text+graphics	192
14		Sum of Page Image	16
15		Sum of Total Views/Database	829
16	North Carolina Newsstand	Sum of Citations	6
17		Sum of Abstracts	150
18		Sum of Text Only	13056
19		Sum of Text+graphics	0
20		Sum of Page Image	0
21		Sum of Total Views/Database	13212
22	PA Research II Newspapers	Sum of Citations	35
23		Sum of Abstracts	2197
24		Sum of Text Only	12
25		Sum of Text+graphics	0
26		Sum of Page Image	0
27		Sum of Total Views/Database	2244
28	PA Research II Periodicals	Sum of Citations	363
29		Sum of Abstracts	11104

CONCLUSION

The usage reports received from vendors at this time arrive in a variety of formats. Moreover, each vendor reports similar statistics differently or statistics that are not necessarily compatible across vendors. The study team continues to work with vendors to standardize definitions, generate compatible reports in identical formats, and provide libraries with similar reporting mechanisms (e.g., via the web).

Until a standardized reporting system is in place, however, users can import current usage data into a variety of analysis programs such as Microsoft Excel for analysis purposes. The above tutorial walks users through that process.

RESOURCES ON USING MICROSOFT EXCEL

Gold, Lauramaery. 1998. *The complete idiot's guide to Microsoft Excel 97.* 2nd ed. Indianapolis: Que Corp.

Harvey, Greg. 1997. *Excel 97 for Windows for Dummies.* Foster City, Calif.: IDG Books Worldwide.

Kinkoph, Sherry. 1999. *The complete idiot's guide to Microsoft Excel 2000.* Indianapolis: Que Corp.

Microsoft Corporation. Microsoft office bookstore: Microsoft Excel titles. Online. Available: <http://www1.fatbrain.com/partners/msoffice/excel. asp>

APPENDIX C

Software for Statistics Collection and Analysis

The following is an introductory list to some of the sources of information on software used to collect and analyze data related to electronic resources and services. The list is not comprehensive. The software identified is not a recommended list of software nor is it the only software of potential use. This area is rapidly evolving, so some of the entries may be out of date.

GENERAL STATISTICS SOFTWARE

Statistics.com. Available: <http://www.statistics.com/>

Library-Specific Statistics Collection and Reporting Software

Bibliostat.com Software Company. Bibliostat software. 250 West Center Street, Suite 300, Provo, UT 84601. Phone (800) 427-0028 or (801) 371-9222. Available: <http://www.bibliostat.com/>

"Bibliostat is software that extracts information from your automation system, warehouses it [in an SQL database], and allows you to produce graphical reports . . . " The Bibliostat Suite is used as an aid to collecting and reporting annual survey data. It includes Bibliostat Collect and Bibliostat Connect. Bibliostat Collect is a customized, Internet-enabled software application that assists libraries in collect-

ing, verifying, and submitting annual data. Bibliostat Connect enables libraries to make comparisons between their libraries and others locally and nationally. The program can also use those comparisons to create effective charts and graphs for use in presentations, budget proposals, and monthly reports.

LOG ANALYSIS

Log analysis seeks to understand the usage of World Wide Web pages by using software to examine files of web page transactions created by web server software.

Articles on Log Analysis Software

Almind, Tomas C. and Ingwersen, Peter. 1997. Informetric analyses on the World Wide Web: Methodological approaches to "webometrics." *Journal of Documentation* 53 (Sept.): 404-426.

Bertot, John Carlo, McClure, Charles R., Moen, William E., and Rubin, Jeffrey. 1997. Web usage statistics: Measurement issues and analytical techniques. *Government Information Quarterly* 14(4): 373-395.

Cirillo, Dominic. 1996. Evaluating website access. Available: <http://trochim.human.cornell.edu/webeval/weblog/weblog.htm> Ithaca, N.Y.: Cornell University.

Dahn, Michael. 2000. Counting angels on a pinhead: Critically interpreting web size estimates. *Online* 24 (1): 35-36+.

McGlamery, Patrick. 1997. MAGIC transaction logs as measures of access, use, and community. *Journal of Academic Librarianship* 23 (6): 505-510.

Morris, Charlie. 1999. There's gold in them thar log files. Available: <http://www.wdvl.com/Internet/Management/index.html>

Mullins, James L. 1999. Statistical measures of usage of web-based resources (developed by the ALA Web Statistics Task Force; presented at the 1998 NASIG Conference). *Serials Librarian* 36: (1-2), 207-210.

Musciano, Chuck. 1996. Collecting and using server statistics. Available: <http://www.sunworld.com/swol-03-1996/swol-03-webmaster.html> What browser are you designing for? Available: <http://www.sunworld.com/swol-03-1996/swol-03-webmaster.html> Analyzing your referrer log. Available: <http://www.sunworld.com/swol-05-1996/swol-05-webmaster. html>

Peters, Thomas A. 1996. Using transaction log analysis for library management information. *Library Administration and Management* 10 (1): 20-25.

Trochim, William M. K. 1996. Evaluating websites. Available: <http://trochim.human.cornell.edu/web eval/webeval.htm> Ithaca, N.Y.: Cornell University.

Log Analysis Software Directories

Boutell, Thomas. WWW FAQ: How can I keep statistics about my web server? Available: <http://www.shu.edu/about/WWWFaq/stats.htm>

Mecklermedia. Web usage tools. Available: <http://www.webreference.com/internet/software/usage.html>

Trochim, William M. K. (1996). Evaluating website access statistical analysis packages. Available: <http://trochim.human.cornell.edu/webeval/weblog/statpack.htm> Ithaca, N.Y.: Cornell University.

Uppsala University. IT Support. Access log analyzers. Available: <http://www.uu.se/Software/Analyzers/Access-analyzers.html>

Web Developer's Virtual Library (WDVL). Statistics. Available: <http://www.wdvl.com/Vlib/Software/Statistics.html>

Yahoo! Computers and the Internet: Log analysis tools. Available: <http://www.yahoo.com/Computers_and_Internet/Software/Internet/World_Wide_Web/Servers/Log_Analysis_Tools>

Specific Log Analysis Software

Accrue Software. Hit List Professional. Available: <http://www.pnw.accrue.com/reporter/reporter.html>

Elron Software. Elron Internet manager. Available: <http://www.elronsoftware.com/enterprise/internet_manager.html> Phone (800) 767-6683, (781) 993-6000; Fax (781) 993-6001

MediaHouse Software Inc. Statistics server. Available: <http://www.mediahouse.com/> 15 Gamelin Blvd., Suite 510, Hull, PQ J8Y 1V4. Canada. Phone (819) 776-0707; Fax (819) 776-5560

Microsoft. Site server. Available: <http://www.microsoft.com/siteserver/site/default.htm> Phone (503) 294-7025

Netgenesis, Inc. Net.Analysis. Available: <http://www.netgenesis.com/products/netanalysis/index.shtml> 150 Cambridge Park Drive, Cambridge, MA 02140. Phone (800) 982-6351, (617) 665-9200; Fax 617-665-9299

Turner, Stephen. Analog. Available: <http://www.statslab.cam.ac.uk/~sret1/analog/> University of Cambridge Statistical Laboratory

WebManage Technologies, Inc. NetIntellect. Available: <http://www.webmanage.com/> Phone (603) 594-9226

Webtrends. Available: <http://www.webtrends.com/default.htm> Phone (503) 294-7025

WRQ. SiteScope. Available: <http://www.wrqwam.com/prodserv/sitescope/> Phone (800) 872-2829, (206) 217-7100

Computer Lab Monitoring and Reservations

Pharos. Sign-up for library PCs. Available: <http://www.pharos.com/>

SRI Strategic Resources, Inc. Library online booking system. Available: <http://www.sri.bc.ca/library.htm>

Silton-Bookman Systems, Inc. Registrar. Available: <http://www.siltonbookman.com/about.html> Stevens Creek Blvd., Suite D, Cupertino, CA 95014-2210.

One feature of this larger software module provides an automated way of determining how much user and staff instruction is provided in a computer lab or cluster.

Computer Usage Monitors and Timers

This type of software tracks the usage at each workstation, often by monitoring keystrokes for words or patterns of data entry. For example, the software can be configured to count how many times users choose each option in an on-screen menu.

Guides

Albrecht, Jack. Computer timers: Specs and evaluation. Available: <http://home.earthlink.net/~coyote8/timers.htm>

Boyle, Padraic. 1995. Buyer's guide: Application metering tools. *PC Magazine* 21 November, 260-261.

Web4Lib. The library web manager's reference center. Timers and session monitors. Available: <http://sunsite.berkeley.edu/Web4Lib/RefCenter/lwmrcpublic.html#timers>

Articles

Colowick, Susan. Who's on first? Assigning Internet computers. Available: <http://www.todayslibrarian.com/articles/9c1desk.html>

Schneider, Karen G. 1999. Safe from prying eyes: Protecting library systems. Available: <http://www.ala.org/alonline/netlib/il199.html>

———. 1998. So they won't hate the wait: Time control for workstations. Available: <http://www.ala.org/alonline/netlib/il1298.html>

Specific Software

Akrontech. Enuff. Available: <http://www.akrontech.com/> 7305 Woodbine Ave., Suite 620, Markham, ON L3R 3V7 Canada. Phone (905) 763-2535; Fax: (905) 763-1350.

Bardon Data Systems. Full Control. Available: <http://www. bardon.com/fullctl.htm> 1164 Solano Ave., Suite #415, Albany, CA 94706. Phone (800) 922-2736; Fax (510) 526-1271.

Bardon Software. WinU. Available: <http://www.bardon.com/>

Computers by Design. CybraryN. Available: <http://www.cybraryn.com/products/cybraryn> 325 Middle Country Road, Suite 6, Selden, NY 11784. Phone (800) THE-TOWN, (516) 696-0700; Fax (516) 696-0950.

Elron Software. SofTrack Software Metering. Available: <http://208.226.13.232/stindex.html> Phone (800) 767-6683, (781) 993-6000; Fax (781) 993-6001.

Fortres Grand Company. Historian. Available: <http://www.fortres.com/> P.O. Box 888, Plymouth, IN 46563. Phone (800) 331-0372; Fax (800) 882-4381.

Hoffmann, Philipp. TimeWatcher. Available: <http://download.cnet.com/downloads/0-10106-100-897913.html?st.dl.search.results.tdtl>

Hypertec. Winselect. Available: <http://www.hypertec.com/>

Invortex Technologies. Public Access Manager (PAM). Available: <http://www.invortex.com/> 1728 Seminole Trail, Suite B, Charlottesville, VA 22901. Phone (804) 975-2152.

Jansma, Nic. WatchDog. Available: <http://download.cnet.com/downloads/0-10105-108-26732.html?tag=st.dl.10105.upd.10105-108-26732>

MR Phelps Ent. Web Time. Available: <http://download.cnet.com/downloads/0-10062-100-882532.html?st.dl.search.results.tdtl>

Network Associates. Site Meter. Available: <http://www.sitemeter.com/>

Novell Inc. Border Manager. Available: <http://www.novell.com/bordermanager/>

Pearl Software. Cybersnoop. Available: <http://www.your-it.com/snoop.htm> Phone (573) 348-3347

Wise Guys. TimeKeeper. Available: <http://download.cnet.com/downloads/0-10106-100-881561.html?st.dl.search.results.tdtl>

Using Nonlibrary-Produced Statistics:
A Bibliography

Data collected by libraries can be combined with data collected by a range of nonlibrary sources to further add value and utility.

Library Research Service. 1999. Community analysis resources on the <http://www.lrs.org/html/community_analysis_resources_o.html>

A model for incorporating nonlibrary-produced data relevant to public libraries.

Library Research Service. Available data for library managers. Available: <http://www.lrs.org/html/available_data_for_library_man.html>

A good start toward identifying key nonlibrary-produced statistics relevant to public libraries.

The Delaware State Library recently commissioned two useful studies that make appropriate use of nonlibrary data:

Loessner, G. Arno and Fanjoy, Ellen H. 1996. *Excellence in public libraries: A program to achieve better information and learning opportunities for Delawareans.* Newark: University of Delaware, College of Urban Affairs and Public Policy, Delaware Public Administration Institute.

Loessner, G. Arno and Fanjoy, Ellen H. 1996. *Improving public libraries in Delaware: An analysis of county-level public library systems.* 2nd ed. Newark: University of Delaware, College of Urban Affairs and Public Policy, Delaware Public Administration Institute.

Examples of interesting use of nonlibrary data in the library literature include:

Seavey, Charles A. 1989. The public library in society: The relationship of libraries and socioeconomic condition. *Public Libraries* 28 (Jan./Feb.): 47-54.

O'Connor, Daniel O. and Fortenbaugh, Robert. 1999. Socioeconomic indicators and library use. *Public Libraries* (May/June): 156-164.

REFERENCES

Adcock, Donald C. 1999. *A planning guide for Information Power: Building partnerships for learning with school library media program assessment rubric for the twenty-first century*. Chicago, American Association of School Librarians, American Library Association.

Babbie, Earl R. 1990. *Survey research methods*. 2nd ed. Belmont, Calif.: Wadsworth.

Bertot, John Carlo and McClure, Charles R. 1998. Measuring electronic services in public libraries: Issues and recommendations. *Public Libraries* 37(3): 176-180.

Bradburn, Frances Bryant. 1999. *Output measures for school library media programs*. New York: Neal Schuman.

Fink, Arlene, ed. 1995. *The survey kit*. Thousand Oaks, Calif.: Sage. For similar titles, see <http://www. sagepub.com/>

Glitz, Beryl. 1997. The focus group technique in library research: An introduction. *Medical Library Association Bulletin* 85 (4): 385-390. Available: <http://www.allenpress.com/mla/issues/vol85/number4/85-4-385.html>

Hafner, Arthur W. 1998. *Descriptive statistical techniques for librarians*. Chicago: American Library Association.

Hernon, Peter. 1989. Research and the use of statistics for library decision making. *Library Administration & Management* 3 (4): 176-180.

Himmel, Ethel and Wilson, Bill. 1998. *Planning for results: A public library transformation process*. Chicago: American Library Association.

Hutton, Bruce and Walters, Suzanne. 1988. Focus groups: Linkages to the community. *Public Libraries* 27 (fall): 149-152.

International Coalition of Library Consortia (ICOLC). 1998. Guidelines for statistical measures of usage of web-based indexed, abstracted, and full text resources. *Information Technology and Libraries* 17 (4): 219-221. See also <http://www.library.yale.edu/consortia/webstats.html>

International Organization for Standardization. (ISO). 2000. *ISO/CD 2789 information and documentation—international library statistics*. Stockholm: Swedish General Standards Institute.

Katzer, Jeffrey, Cook, Kenneth H., and Crouch, Wayne W. 1998. *Evaluating information: A guide for users of social science research*. 4th ed. Boston: McGraw-Hill.

Krueger, Richard A. 1994. *Focus groups: A practical guide for applied research*. Newbury Park, Calif.: Sage.

Library Research Service. 1995. *Circulation statistics: What's excluded? Fast facts: Recent statistics from the Library Research Service*, 3/1.0.10/, no. 96 (Feb. 23).

Loessner, G. Arno and Fanjoy, Ellen H. 1996. *Improving public libraries in Delaware: An analysis of county-level public library systems*. 2nd ed. Newark: University of Delaware, College of Urban Affairs and Public Policy, Delaware Public Administration Institute.

Mason, Marilyn Gell. 1999. *Strategic management for today's libraries*. Chicago: American Library Association.

Mayo, Diane and Nelson, Sandra. 1999. *Wired for the future: Developing your library technology plan*. Chicago: American Library Association.

McClure, Charles R. and Lopata, Cynthia L. 1996. *Assessing the academic networked environment: Strategies and options*. Washington, D.C.: Coalition for Networked Information.

Moran, Barbara B. 1985. Construction of the questionnaire in survey research. *Public Libraries* 24 (summer): 75-76.

Morgan, David L. 1993. *Successful focus groups: Advancing the state of the art*. Newbury Park, Calif.: Sage.

Nelson, Sandra, Altman, Ellen, and Mayo, Diane. 2000. *Managing for results: Effective resource allocation for public libraries*. Chicago: American Library Association.

Public Library Association. *Public library data service: Statistical report*. Chicago: Public Library Association. American Library Association. Annual.

Ryan, Joe. 1998. Library statistics and performance measures. Available: <http://web.syr.edu/~jryan /infopro/stats. html>

Salant, Priscilla and Dillman, Don A. 1994. *How to conduct your own survey*. New York: Wiley.

Stewart, David W. and Sharcasani, Prem N. 1990. *Focus groups: Theory and practice*. Newbury Park, Calif.: Sage.

Van House, Nancy A., Lynch, Mary Jo, McClure, Charles R., Zweizig, Douglas L., and Rodger, Eleanor Jo. 1987. *Output measures for public libraries: A manual of standardized procedures*. 2nd ed. Chicago: American Library Association.

Walter, Virginia A. 1995. *Output measures and more: Planning and evaluating public library services for young adults*. Chicago: American Library Association.

———. 1992. *Output measures for public library service to children: A manual of standardized procedures*. Chicago: American Library Association.

INDEX

John Carlo Bertot <jcbertot@lis.fsu.edu> is associate professor in the School of Information Studies and associate director of the Information Use Management and Policy Institute at Florida State University <http://www.ii.fsu.edu/>. He was the co-principal investigator for the National Leadership Grant funded by the Institute of Museum and Library Services to develop national public library statistics and performance measures for the networked environment that made this manual possible. Bertot continues to work with public and other libraries to develop, plan, and evaluate network-based services through a variety of projects. He is also the president of Bertot Information Consultant Services, Inc. Additional information on Bertot is available at <http://slis-two. lis.fsu.edu/~jcbertot/>.

Charles R. McClure is the Francis Eppes Professor of Information Studies <cmcclure@lis.fsu.edu> and director of the Information Use Management and Policy Institute at Florida State University. McClure has written extensively on topics related to planning and evaluation of information services, information resources management, and federal information policy. He is the co-editor of *Evaluating Networked Information Services* (Information Today, 2000) and president of Information Management Consulting Services, Inc. Additional information about McClure can be found at <http://slis-two.lis.fsu.edu/~ cmcclure/>.

Joe Ryan <jryan@mailbox.syr.edu> assists librarians in evaluating their network services. He was project coordinator for the IMLS-funded study enabling the research for this book and for evaluating the California State Library's InfoPeople project as well as the on-site evaluator for a Department of Education grant to the Portland (Oreg.) Area Library System (PORTALS). Ryan is director of Ryan Information Management. For additional information, see <http://web.syr.edu/~jryan/index.html>.